# The Scottish-Irish Pub and Hearth Cookbook

# The Scottish-Irish Pub and Hearth Cookbook

### Recipes and Lore from Celtic Kitchens

KAY SHAW NELSON

HIPPOCRENE BOOKS, INC.
New York

Paperback edition, 2009

For information, address:
HIPPOCRENE BOOKS, INC.
171 Madison Avenue
New York, NY 10016
www.hippocrenebooks.com


ISBN-13: 978-0-7818-1241-2 (pb)
ISBN-10: 0-7818-1241-0 (pb)

ISBN-13: 978-0-7818-0741-8 (hb)
ISBN-10: 0-7818-0741-7 (hb)


Printed in the United States of America.

*To the memory of my Scottish forebears,*
*the Morrisons, MacLeods, MacAskills and Shaws*
*and to*
*my Celtic friends,*
*especially the Scots and Irish*

# ACKNOWLEDGMENTS

First, I wish to thank my daughter, Rae, for her continual support, excellent ideas, editorial, and technical assistance.

Second, my grateful thanks to all the people who believe that the food of a nation is part of its history and culture and maintain that this information is very important.

Over the years, many friends and acquaintances have helped me considerably in my quest for Scottish and Irish as well as Celtic knowledge, including history, folklore, lifestyles, and cooking. This began during my childhood in Lebanon, New . Hampshire, where I learned about my Scottish heritage from my parents, Dolina MacAskill and Angus Shaw, and their sisters and brothers. During visits to my parents' beloved homeland, the small isle of Cape Breton off the Nova Scotian mainland, my Canadian relatives introduced me to the delight and goodness of homemade Scottish fare. I thank them and all the friendly Scots and Irish who provided hospitality, helpful talks, and recipes during my travels in Scotland and Ireland. Celts everywhere are noted for their conviviality and sharing of food and drink.

I also thank my neighbors and friends who have been kind enough to share meals with me during the testing of my recipes. Their reactions and comments were appreciated.

I wish to thank particularly the Scottish and Irish Tourist Boards for their valuable information and guidance. And, also, Carol Chitnis, Managing Editor of Hippocrene Books for her helpful suggestions throughout the writing of this book.

# CONTENTS

# PREFACE

It was a glorious June evening in Tarbert, an ancient fishing port beautifully situated at the northern tip of the long, narrow Kintyre Peninsula, almost an island between the waters of the Firth of Clyde and the Atlantic. Travelling alone in Scotland to experience Scottish lifestyles and to refresh my mind and body, I had arrived by happenstance in Mid Argyll, the ancient heartland of the land of the Gael, an unspoiled and beautiful area with a wide range of historical and vacation sites to visit.

After checking into a hotel centrally located on the waterfront overlooking the harbor and hills of Knapdale beyond, there was time to look for local food specialties. I always travel with culinary subjects in mind, and I'm usually rewarded with one or more discoveries that leave everlasting impressions.

In Tarbert I would not be disappointed. I bought little jars of unusual Arran Island mustards, Campbeltown cheeses, and freshly baked breads. Restaurant and café menus advertised sweet queen scallops, Arran cod, prawns, salmon, mussels, cockles, and pickled herring for dinner. Fish bars sold langoustines, whiting, plaice, and mackerel. At Take Aways, a sidewalk store, one could buy fried haddock or scampi, savory pies and puddings. A fishmonger proffered salmon smoked on the shores of Loch Fyne and cured with Glenturret, a curious but likeable Tayside whisky with a light lemony flavor.

The next morning, after a characteristic hearty Scottish breakfast, I set out to view Tarbert's castles but was soon drawn to the waterfront of the picturesque almost landlocked harbor surrounded by fishermen's cottages, shops and hostelries. I am always hard put to choose between the historic attractions and those related to food, the objects of most of my trips. The temptations of both usually prove irresistible. Fortunately, it's often possible to combine my two major travel interests. I had found an ideal locale for this.

Although I was in Scotland many of the foods reminded me of those I had enjoyed in Ireland. On my previous extended sojourns in the Highlands and Islands and visits in the Emerald Isle, I'd become increasingly interested in the similarities between and appeal of Scottish and Irish foods, drinks, culinary arts, and holiday celebrations. But it was not until my stopover in Kintyre that the Gaelic traditions of good eating, convivial entertaining, and congeniality crystallized as I learned about remarkable places and sagas of the past.

The west coast of Scotland from Tarbert to the tip of Kintyre is one of the most interesting and spectacular corners of Scotland and has long had a close affinity with neighboring Ireland through cultural and economic links. The peninsula, only about twelve miles from the Irish north coast, is ancient Dalriada, the first kingdom of the Scots, from where they migrated north to Argyll. An early center of Christianity in Scotland, legend has it that St. Columba—in Gaelic Columcille, "dove of the church,"— first set foot in the country near the present holiday Southend village, at Keil Point to the east of Carskey Bay, in 561 A.D. This was before he went on to Iona. Kintyre also has a rich sculptural heritage of ancient standing stones, Christian sites, and reminders of the Celtic Iron Age.

Both Scotland and Ireland have histories involving strife and struggles, captivating natural beauty, romantic legends, tenacious people, notable drink, and hearty dishes strongly linked to a deep sense of tradition, individualism and hospitality, dating back to Celtic times, and based primarily on a wealth of superior natural resources. The Scots and Irish have long enjoyed nourishing, simple fare that evolved over the centuries from a thrifty, wholesome diet to, in recent times, a more diverse one tied to continental influences.

Scotland, or Caledonia, was at first an isolated land inhabited by Picts, the earliest Celtic Britons of obscure origin, who were given that name because of the way that they pricked or tattooed their bodies, and settled there in pre-Christian times. Then, between the 3$^{rd}$ and 6$^{th}$ centuries, came successive waves of Celts from Ireland who established a new homeland across the sea. They were known as Scotti or Scots and brought their Gaelic language and customs, including a method of baking on a griddle or "girdle" that gave birth to the Scottish repertoire of versatile daily breads.

One major difference between the development of the Scottish and Irish cuisines, however, is that the former owes a great deal to the French, who formed an Auld Alliance with the Scots, beginning in the 13$^{th}$ century as allies against the English. Long years of association with France added many refinements to the basic dishes. The Scottish nobility's style of living was greatly influenced by the French court. Scottish cooking, goes the saying, is a "pastoral one that went to Paris and took on French airs."

Ironically, Ireland's traditional cookery has taken on new meaning through the country's late 20$^{th}$ century culinary alliance with France. Today's "Modern Irish Cuisine" was started under the guidance of Myrtle Allen, Ireland's best known gastronomic authority, and is continued by her daughter-in-law, Darina, of the Ballymaloe House and Cookery School in County Cork. It has been enhanced by young Irish chefs, many of them trained in French culinary schools and restaurants. Utilizing Ireland's first-class native ingredients and cooking them simply but imaginatively, these men and women turn out innovative dishes in their homeland's various eating and dining establishments.

Today in Scotland and Ireland the patterns of cooking and dining are changing as exotic foreign foods and dishes are continuously introduced. Both countries have excellent natural resources, especially seafood, meat, game, and dairy products. And vegetable production and consumption are increasing. Fortunately, there is still an interest in traditional fare as well as the culinary creations of contemporary cooks.

My collection of recipes is selective rather than comprehensive, and is intended to present distinctive and delectable examples of the past and present Scottish and Irish cuisines.

I hope that it will evoke pleasant memories for those who have travelled in these countries. Others may savor and appreciate the intriguing variety of the best from Celtic kitchens designed for informal good times.

# INTRODUCTION

There's a great tradition of merrymaking in Scotland and Ireland. Both countries are famous for their spirit of hospitality. I believe it's fair to say that there exists in almost every Gaelic soul the desire to have a good time at a gathering of congenial people who can relax, talk, perhaps sing or dance, drink, and enjoy plenty of joyous eating. The Gaels bring to the table a natural respect for fine food and festivity.

Although seldom acclaimed for their culinary expertise, the Scots and Irish are instinctive, genuine cooks, having what may be called a "lucky hand." A favorite food, goes the saying, is the "better for the cooking of it." Dear to their hearts is the cornucopia of flavorful ingredients grown and harvested locally. From earliest times, the peoples of these lands retained a stubborn preference for their simple, hearty, nutritious fare made with recipes passed from one generation to the next.

The Gaelic tradition of food culture dates back to the Celts, an ancient people who migrated westward from an area east of the river Rhine and north of the Alps. Celts have been called "the first Europeans." Brilliant, practical, courageous, superstitious, and most inventive, they were primarily a farming people and groups of them would set out to find new lands where they could form permanent settlements. They had herding and fishing societies, and grew garden crops.

Staples of the diet were grains, vegetables, cheeses, and some meat, especially pork. The Celts did all their cooking over open fires, preparing tender cuts of meat by roasting them upon spits and tougher cuts by stewing them with grains and herbs. To cook soups and stews, Celts devised round-bottomed metal cauldrons that could be placed directly over or suspended above the flames. For making bread, they milled flour with querns, and baked flat cakes of dough in a type of simple oven made by

1

inverting a pot over them as they rested on hot stones in the fire. Some breads were made lighter by the addition of beer as a kind of leavening.

Celts are believed to have come in the 6th century B.C. to the eastern Atlantic seaboard—Ireland and the highlands and islands of Scotland. Here, in an area that never came under Roman rule or influence, they established proud Celtic nations and left an intricate legacy of culture, language and hospitality that survives today through music, songs, dances, and story-telling. Cooking is also an integral part of the heritage.

The Gaelic Celts had a highly organized social structure that included strict rules concerning meals and entertaining set down by the Brehon Laws, formulated about 438 A.D. They also brought to these lands important foods—vinegar, salt, honey, and a wild cabbage closely akin to kale, among others—and introduced the techniques of making butter, handmilling flour for bread, herbal cultivation, and basic culinary skills.

According to chronicles and legend, the Celts lived in iso-lated farmsteads and were generous and friendly, ever ready to welcome strangers and give them food and drink. The deep rooted tradition of hospitality and sociability in the Gaelic cul-ture dates back to the Celts.

Like most people who lived in remote communities, they devised their own entertainment, spending evenings eating and drinking while listening to music and telling stories by firesides long into the night. Spontaneous gatherings in one or another of their homes became a way of life. No matter how humble a dwelling might be, there was always room for the family and vis-itors to gather around the hearth, the focal point of the home—a center of domestic and social activities and symbol of hospitality. Music was played, songs sung, poems recited, tall tales told, and all were welcome.

Traditional Gaelic social gatherings, dating from those early magical evenings, are the Scottish *ceilidh* and Irish *ceili*, words for "visit." Although a "wee" *ceilidh* can be only two people—one person dropping in on another for a gossipy chat—the occasion is by definition more typically an informal get-together of several persons in a home or public hall with music and food. Over the years the gatherings have been slowly formalized into exhilarating social events with spirited dancing to tunes played on traditional instruments. Increasingly throughout Scotland and Ireland, hotels, clubs and restaurants offer visitors an opportunity to join in the good times or to observe the dances and listen to the music or Gaelic floor shows, often with dinner and drinks.

A fondness for robust festivities also dates back to the Celts. From the earliest times they loved to celebrate a birthday, victory in battle, and, especially a religious festival, with a feast—an occasion for rejoicing with hearty food, copious drinks, and merriment. Because the Celtic year was divided into four parts according to seasons, the passage from one to the other was marked by a lively festival, observed with ceremony and frivolity commemorating the activities of the farming year.

*Samhain* (pronounced Sow'en), celebrated on November 1st, the Celtic New Year, marked the end of the harvest season and beginning of winter. It was an occasion for carousing and consuming large quantities of roasted meat. Because *Samhain* is when the earth rests and fertility is renewed, the holiday came to be associated with all kinds of superstitions, including ghosts and ghouls. Later, in Christian times, many of the observances were transferred to the night before, All Hallow's Eve or Halloween.

The festival of *Imbolc*, the first day of spring and the beginning of the new year on the farm, celebrated on February 1st, was dedicated to Brigit, goddess of all creative activity. Now St. Bridget's Day, observed on the same date, honors the much-loved Irish saint from early Christian times. *Beltaine* or May Day, May 1, when the year begins its bright summer half, originally was to hail the sown fields starting to sprout, but it became an occasion for singing and dancing and, in some locales, it was the custom to cut down a hawthorn tree to use as a Maypole. The holiday was also celebrated with bonfires to scare away the witches in the sky, and the cattle being driven to open grazing.

The most joyous of the quarterly festivals was *Lughnasa*, the harvest feast of the great god Lugh, still celebrated on August 1<sup>st</sup>. It was marked by rituals to ensure a successful harvest, pageants, and various communal pastimes—sporting events, singing, dancing, and eating gargantuan meals.

Over the years the Scots and Irish created many imaginative dishes and drinks for their festivals and these recipes have been handed down through generations. The Gaels have a flair for celebrating their treasured holidays and show respect for their heritage and ancient traditions in many ways, but especially with a festive meal.

Another popular Gaelic way of socializing is to drop in at a favorite pub for a chat, to argue, wisecrack, laugh, eat, and, especially, to drink! The word "pub" is a shortened version of "public house." Scotland and Ireland have plentiful pubs of every description, bearing every conceivable name, and seemingly around every corner. The pub is an integral part of Gaelic life that caters to everyone's tastes. For centuries the quaint and picturesque tavern, local, or just plain pub, has been a home away from home for the Scots and Irish. Call it what you will, it's a friendly watering hole with a lyrical name, lots of atmosphere, and a place where you can chase the blues away, enjoy a chummy dart game, criticize the politicians, and order up a pint of lager or black foamy stout, an interesting and distinctive brew.

The Gaels have a favorite saying: "Laughter is gayest when the hunger is best." And, indeed, they love to sit and enjoy their "pub grub," as the tempting casual fare has been dubbed. Pub grub is time-tested, satisfying, cheery, and homey food that usually includes a good variety of regional and national dishes such as hearty soups, savory pies, rib-sticking stews, clever potato

4

creations, country hams, flavorful seafood, and a great variety of baked goods with inventive names. What is sometimes lacking in variety is made up for in the deliciousness of the fresh and excellent food.

The simple but satisfying pub fare grew out of serving people food and drink efficiently and practically in a congenial atmosphere. It is ideal for home family meals and entertaining. The dishes are attractive, easy to prepare, economical, can be made partially or totally ahead, and, needless to say, are delectable.

It is no coincidence that one of the best known of all Gaelic phrases is *"Ceud Mile Failte"* which means "A Hundred Thousand Welcomes," an apt expression of hospitality which rings through all convivial gatherings.

As you will discover, this book is about cooking but it's also about having a good time. It offers suggestions and recipes for many tastes. Selections have been made to provide fare that is not only appealing but an interesting variation on the usual culinary repertoire. I hope that both the text and recipes will enhance the pleasure of cooking and serving this marvelous food as the Celtic, or Gaelic, spirit of conviviality lives on.

# Starters

*Standing Stones of Callanish, Isle of Lewis.*

7

*"Food should be eaten as fresh as possible while drink should be well matured."*

— *An old Gaelic adage*

Initially it was family tree curiosity that drew me to Scotland's Isle of Lewis, the largest and most northerly of the Outer Hebrides, a remote area of stunning scenery, wild beauty, and warm welcomes. My forebears, the Morrisons, MacLeods, MacAskills and Shaws, left for America in the mid-1800s from here. But, as is my habit, I took time to explore and enjoy the local culinary specialties and libations.

After a day spent tracing ancestors, and exploring the Standing Stones of Callanish, an unearthly setting of megaliths said to have been used by the ancients to track moon movements, I took refuge from the rain in a pub. Fortunately, hospitality thrives in Stornoway, the island's lively port and tweed-spinning town, so, by evening, I was enjoying a wee dram and dining extremely well on smoked fish, oatcakes, and crowdie, a soft white cheese.

Here, as in all Gaelic locales, leisurely sampling of tempting and satisfying foods, fresh or preserved, with drinks is an end of the day tradition. In cozy retreats, twilight is the time to relax with a single malt, stout, or another brew, and while the time away sipping, eating, chatting, and taking in the scene.

Colorful and tasty appetizers, or starters as the Gaels say, are served as tidbits or first-course food. They include an appealing choice of seafood delights as well as other treats. I eagerly enjoyed them all during my Gaelic travels.

# ❀ SMOKED SALMON

Prime Scottish and Irish smoked salmon, beautifully textured and perfectly cured, is an exceptional delicacy, especially enjoyable with drinks before a meal. While the salmon originally may be wild or farmed, it is smoked by a process that leads to uniquely flavored fish.

True Scottish smoked salmon is processed through a superior cold smoking technique using various combinations of salt, brown sugar, spices, and rum, whisky or Drambuie. The final product has a pale reddish-orange color, firm texture with a glossy sheen, and a smoky, slightly salty flavor.

For centuries Ireland's succulent salmon has been smoked with the wood of oak trees, following a tradition that enhances the natural oils and goodness of the fish. According to legend this ancient delicacy was left by Druids as an offering to Dagda, Gaelic god of the earth. And it is believed that the salmon was served at Tara, seat of the High Kings of Ireland, for a 5th century banquet.

Most Gaels prefer the smoked salmon *au naturel*, without accompaniments. Serve each person a few cold, thin slices (cut diagonally as close to serving time as possible), with a wedge of lemon and thinly sliced buttered or plain brown bread.

For easy starters, coil thin strips of smoked salmon into rounds shaped like "roses" and place on buttered brown bread squares. Or, serve thin salmon slices on oatcakes or brown soda bread, garnished with sour cream and chopped fresh dill.

Here are two other suggestions for salmon starters.

# ❀ TOBERMORY SMOKED SALMON PÂTÉ

"The Fish with the Hebridean Flavor" comes from Tobermory, on the Isle of Mull, a charming fishing village where the exceptional cold bay water results in farmed salmon of superior quality. Silky and succulent with a unique tang of spices and wood-smoke, it blends well with a few ingredients for this pâté.

½ cup (1 stick) unsalted butter, softened
3 tablespoons dairy sour cream
1 teaspoon fresh lemon juice
Freshly ground white or black pepper
3 tablespoons minced scallions, with some pale green tops
¼ cup diced smoked salmon
Fresh watercress leaves

In a medium bowl cream the butter until light and fluffy. Add sour cream and lemon juice. Season with pepper. Beat again. Stir in scallions and salmon. Mix to blend well. Refrigerate, covered with plastic wrap, at least 2 hours and up to 2 days. Serve in a mound on a plate. Garnish with watercress leaves. Makes 1 cup.

# ✸ LISDOONVARNA CHEESE-FILLED SALMON CONES

At the Barren Smokehouse in the spa town of Lisdoonvarna, County Clare, visitors can learn about the ancient tradition of oat-smoking salmon, and, at the Roadside Tavern, enjoy an unusual toasted sandwich made with white bread, filled with home-smoked salmon, tomato and onion slices. Here's a good smoked salmon starter named for the colorful town which hosts a merry annual September Matchmaking Festival, inspired, they say, by the invigorating local waters and traditional revelries.

1 package (8 ounces) cream cheese, softened
1 cup dairy sour cream
1 tablespoon prepared horseradish, drained
3 tablespoons minced chives
1 teaspoon sugar
Salt, freshly ground white or black pepper
12 4-inch squares thinly sliced smoked salmon

In a medium bowl whisk the cheese. Add the sour cream, horseradish, chives, and sugar. Season with salt and pepper. Stir until smooth. Cover with plastic wrap. Refrigerate for 2 hours, up to 2 days. To prepare, place 2 to 3 tablespoons of cream cheese mixture along the center of each salmon square, dividing evenly. Roll into cone shapes. Fasten with toothpicks. Arrange on a plate. Refrigerate, covered with plastic wrap, up to 4 hours. Makes 12.

# ❀ GALWAY BAY OYSTERS

*". . . the Celts gathered oysters and fed on them abundantly."*

— *Larousse Gastronomy*

Although there are any number of Gaelic locales where oysters are particularly fancied, one of my favorite places is Galway City, an ancient capital and lively trading center with winding streets, broad quays, medieval houses, and lots of merriment. Here its prized sea delicacy is honored with an annual September Oyster Festival attracting thousands of celebrants who devour enormous quantities of the small, succulent oysters and wash them down with gallons of stout, and jokes and stories.

"If you get enough Irishmen drinking and talking, that's a festival in itself," goes an old saying. And, at the Galway celebration one finds plenty of both. There's no more pleasant place to be awed with oystermania than in this grown-up fishing village eating lots of cool, briny oysters, and at evening gazing out upon the romantic Galway Bay. For here's where "Earth's most charismatic mollusk" is accorded a glorious gala.

Gaels prefer to eat their oysters raw on the half shell, served on a bed of cracked ice, and perhaps seaweed, with a lemon wedge, buttered brown bread, and stout on the side. They also can be prepared as follows.

# ❀ OYSTER PAN ROAST

When entertaining a wee group at a festive home party, serve these oysters-on-the-half-shell with a plate of raw vegetables, a bowl of watercress leaves, and buttered soda bread.

24 oysters on the half shell
8 slices thin bacon
⅓ cup minced scallions
⅓ cup minced green pepper
½ cup chopped fresh parsley
Juice of 1 large lemon

Preheat oven to 450 degrees.

Take oysters from shells; scrub shells with a wire brush to remove any sand. Return oysters to shells. Place on a baking sheet.

In a small skillet fry the bacon over medium-high heat to partially cook, or until it is translucent. Remove from skillet; cut each slice into three pieces; set aside. Add scallions and green pepper to bacon fat; sauté 1 minute. Spoon vegetable mixture over oysters, dividing evenly. Top each oyster with a piece of bacon and sprinkling of lemon juice. Roast in preheated oven until oysters are hot and bacon is crisp. Serve at once. 4 servings. (These can be partially prepared ahead, refrigerated, and cooked just before serving.)

# ✸ ANGELS ON HORSEBACK

A number of piquant starters, once served as savouries or appetizing morsels after dinner, have amusing names such as this one. It's prepared with two great Irish foods, oysters (also called angels) and bacon, that are cooked together and served at unpretentious and fashionable pubs as well as in the home.

12 large shucked raw oysters
Juice of 1 lemon
Freshly ground pepper
Paprika
6 slices thin bacon
12 small rounds of buttered brown bread

Preheat oven to 500 degrees.

Drain oysters. Sprinkle with lemon juice, a little pepper and paprika. Cut each bacon slice crosswise in half. Wrap each oyster with bacon; secure ends with a toothpick. Arrange oysters in a pan. Cook, turning once, in preheated oven until bacon is crisp and brown but oysters remain juicy, about 6 minutes. Serve each one (toothpicks removed) on a bread round. Makes 12.

# ❀ TARBERT KIPPER PÂTÉ

One of best Gaelic seafood specialties is kippers, or kippered herring, herrings that are split open, flattened, then lightly salted and smoked. Although associated primarily with Scotland, they are also enjoyed by the Irish in a number of dishes. "Scotland's finest" kippers come from Loch Fyne, a westerly loch sheltered by the Mull of Kintrye, long celebrated for its gleaming plump herring, full of fat and flavor. A good place to enjoy kippers is at Tarbert, especially during the annual five-day Seafood Festival at the beginning of July.

Here's a recipe for an easy, tasty spread made with canned kipper fillets.

2 cans (3¼ ounces each) kipper fillets, drained, cut up
½ cup (1 stick) unsalted butter, softened, cut in small pieces
2 tablespoons fresh lemon juice
2 teaspoons minced onion
1 teaspoon minced chives
2 teaspoons Dijon-style mustard
Freshly ground pepper

In a blender or food processor, with metal blade in place, purée kippers, butter, lemon juice, onion, chives, and mustard with pepper to taste. Spoon mixture into an earthenware or glass container. Leave at room temperature 30 minutes. Refrigerate, covered with plastic wrap, several hours, up to 4 days. Serve with thin slices of brown bread or oatcakes. Makes 1½ cups.

*View of Tarbert Harbor.*

# ❀ DUBLIN BAY PRAWN COCKTAIL

A seafood delicacy that comes from Dublin Bay, and is highly prized by the Irish, has been called a prawn but is a variety of lobster. Sweet and tender with a wonderful sea taste, the prawns are best steamed and served with butter and lemon juice or a piquant sauce.

¼ cup whipped heavy cream
¼ cup tomato sauce
Juice of 1 large lemon
1 teaspoon Worcestershire sauce
½ to 1 teaspoon prepared horseradish, drained
Salt and freshly ground pepper
½ cup shredded lettuce
½ cup chopped celery
24 large cleaned, shelled, cooked prawns or shrimps

In a medium bowl combine the cream, tomato sauce, lemon juice, Worcestershire, and horseradish. Season with salt and pepper. Cover with plastic wrap. Refrigerate 1 to 2 hours to blend flavors. When ready to serve for a first course, place the lettuce and celery, dividing evenly, in 4 stemmed glasses. For each serving, arrange 6 prawns or shrimps, and a spoonful of the sauce. As starters, arrange the ingredients on a large plate or platter and pass them. 4 servings.

# ❀ GENTLEMEN'S RELISH

Long ago the tangy, tiny anchovy, a member of the herring family, became an esteemed pub food, delighting the palate as its salty flavor is appealing and stimulates thirst. Most anchovies are sold in cans as fillets, either straight strips or curls. Used to flavor bland foods, they provide zest for many starters.

This 19th century spicy anchovy paste, commonly called Gentlemen's Relish, once served as a savoury, is eaten on hot buttered toast with drinks or tea. Here's my version of it.

2 cans (2 ounces each) anchovy fillets, drained and cut up
½ cup (1 stick) unsalted butter, softened
2 tablespoons fine dry brown bread crumbs
2 tablespoons minced onions
2 teaspoons Dijon-style mustard
¼ teaspoon paprika
4 teaspoons fresh lemon juice
Freshly ground pepper

In a blender or food processor, with metal blade in place, purée anchovies, butter, bread crumbs, onions, mustard, paprika, lemon juice, and pepper to taste. Spoon into a small pot or bowl. Refrigerate, covered with plastic wrap, 2 hours or up to 4 days. Leave at room temperature 30 minutes before serving. To serve, put dish in center of a small plate and surround with squares of brown bread or white toast. Makes 1 cup.

# ❀ SCOTCH EGGS

*"It is inconceivable that my ultimate favorite nosh is that simple creation so typical of the pubs of the British Isles, Scotch eggs . . . I have been addicted to Scotch eggs since I first encountered them while standing at a bar near Glasgow . . . These eggs are, seemingly, one of the most basic concepts of cooking."*

— **Craig Claiborne**

12 hard-cooked eggs
All-purpose flour
2 pounds bulk pork sausage
¼ cup minced onions
¼ cup finely chopped fresh parsley
Salt, freshly ground pepper
3 to 4 large eggs, beaten
About 2 cups fine dry bread crumbs
Vegetable oil for deep-frying

Shell the eggs; wipe dry with paper towels. Roll each one in flour to coat lightly. Set aside.

In a large bowl combine the sausage, onions, and parsley. Season with salt and pepper; mix thoroughly. Divide mixture into 12 equal portions; flatten into thin rounds. Place 1 floured egg in the center of each round; cover completely with sausage, patting it well. Dip in beaten eggs; coat evenly with bread crumbs. Place on a large plate. Cover with plastic wrap and refrigerate, up to 12 hours.

To cook, heat 3 inches of oil in a deep-fryer. Fry eggs, 1 or 2 at a time, turning them, in hot deep oil (325 degrees) until crisp and golden, about 7 minutes. With a slotted spoon, transfer eggs as they are cooked to drain on paper towels.

Serve the eggs hot or chilled, plain or with mustard. Makes 12 whole or 24 halves.

# ❀ ERIN SHRIMP PASTE

This time-honored spread is a good starter to keep ready in the refrigerator for week-end guests.

1 pound cooked, shelled tiny shrimp, deveined
½ cup (1 stick) butter, softened, cut in small pieces
3 tablespoons fresh lemon juice
2 teaspoons Dijon-style mustard
⅛ teaspoon cayenne pepper
¼ teaspoon freshly grated nutmeg
Salt, freshly ground pepper

In a blender or food processor, with metal blade in place, combine the shrimp, butter, lemon juice, mustard, cayenne pepper, nutmeg, with salt and pepper to taste. Process to blend well. Spoon mixture into a small pot, mold or bowl. Refrigerate, covered, up to 3 days. Serve with toast triangles or wheat crackers. Makes about 1½ cups.

# ❀ CALEDONIA MEATBALLS

Caledonia, an ancient poetical name for Scotland, is said to be a corruption of Celyddon, a Celtic word meaning "a dweller in the woods and forests." The word Celt, from the same source, means the same thing.

Meatballs in Caledonia can be traced back to the days when they were called "spoon meat." Since before the introduction of forks, the food could be easily handled with either a spoon or the fingers.

1 cup soft bread cubes
½ cup milk
⅓ cup minced onions
1¼ pounds lean ground beef
1 tablespoon Dijon-style mustard
1 tablespoon Worcestershire sauce
1 tablespoon curry powder
1 tablespoon fresh lemon juice
⅛ to ¼ teaspoon cayenne pepper
1 teaspoon salt
¼ teaspoon freshly ground pepper
Vegetable oil for frying

In a small bowl soak the bread cubes in the milk. Squeeze dry and place in a large bowl. Add the onions, beef, mustard, Worcestershire, curry powder, lemon juice, cayenne, salt, and pepper. Mix thoroughly. Roll mixture a little at a time into small balls. Heat enough oil to cover the bottom of a medium skillet. Fry meatballs, several at a time, turning frequently, until brown on all sides. Drain on paper towels. Serve at once. Or cool and refrigerate. To reheat, place on baking sheet in preheated 400-degree oven for 2 to 3 minutes, turning once or twice. Makes 8 to 9 dozen.

# ❀ SAUSAGES IN PASTRY "COATS"

Most pubs serve sausages in one or more forms as Gaels have a boundless enthusiasm for them. They hold a very special place in the traditional nosher repertoire.

24 link pork sausages
1½ cups all-purpose flour
¾ teaspoon salt
½ cup vegetable shortening, cut in small pieces
About 4 tablespoons cold water
1 large egg, beaten

Preheat oven to 425 degrees. Grease a baking sheet.

In a large skillet partially cook sausages by frying over medium-high to release almost all of the fat. Drain on paper towels; cool.

Into a medium bowl sift the flour and salt. With a pastry blender, cut in shortening until mixture is uniformly crumbly. Add water, 1 tablespoon at a time, enough to make a firm dough. Turn out on a lightly floured surface; roll into a thin rectangle. Cut into 24 strips, each about 2½ × 3 inches. Place a sausage link in center of each strip; roll up, leaving ends of sausage out. Seal pastry edges with a little cold water. Cut a couple of small slashes across top of each roll. Brush tops with beaten egg. Place about 1 inch apart on prepared baking sheet. Bake in preheated oven until pastry is crisp and golden, about 20 minutes. Serve hot or cold with mustard. Makes 24.

# ❀ AYRSHIRE SAUSAGE SQUARES

Ayrshire, a prosperous farming region in southwestern Scotland, known primarily for its association with Robbie Burns, the country's beloved national poet, has a number of high quality pork products. These herb-flavored sausage squares are an adaptation of a starter I enjoyed in an atmospheric village pub where the poet once dropped by for a dram or two.

¾ cup old-fashioned rolled oats
1 package (16 ounces) mild pork sausage
½ cup finely chopped onions
5 large eggs
½ cup grated Parmesan cheese
1 teaspoon dried basil
½ teaspoon dried oregano
⅛ teaspoon freshly ground pepper
2½ cups shredded scraped carrots (about 3 medium)
1½ cups shredded Cheddar cheese (¼ pound)

Preheat oven to 325 degrees. Grease a shallow baking dish (13" × 9" × 2").

Spread oats in a medium ungreased skillet. Toast over medium-high heat, stirring 2 or 3 times, until edges are golden, about 3 minutes. Remove from heat; cool.

In a large skillet fry sausage and onions over medium-high heat, stirring to break up the sausage, until all the redness is gone. Spoon off all the fat.

In a large bowl whisk the eggs. Stir in Parmesan cheese, basil, oregano, and pepper. Gradually stir in the sausage mixture, toasted oats, and carrots, mixing to blend thoroughly. Spoon into prepared dish, spreading evenly. Bake in the preheated oven 25 minutes. Remove from oven; spread top with shredded Cheddar. Return to oven; cook 15 minutes longer. Remove from oven; cool 10 minutes. Cut into 1½-inch squares. Makes about 32.

The squares may be prepared ahead and cooked just before serving. Or, cook; cool; cover and refrigerate. Place in a preheated 325 degree oven until hot, about 20 minutes.

## ❀ SEANACHIE EGG MAYONNAISE

In the days before magazines and television, a man travelling around the Gaelic countryside bringing news and telling tales was called a *seanachie* or storyteller. Over the years much of the Celtic lore, especially about heroic achievements, was passed from one generation to the next by this beloved personality. Consequently, storytelling in Gaelic lands became a respected art and was once a real profession.

The Seanachie Pub, a late 18th century thatched restaurant in a farmyard setting near Dungarvan, Waterford County, is an Irish institution noted for its good food, traditional music and dancing as well as storytelling. This recipe is an adaptation of a favorite Irish starter that I enjoyed there on a bright summer day.

6 hard-cooked eggs, shelled
1 teaspoon Dijon-style mustard
2 tablespoons mayonnaise
1 tablespoon finely chopped watercress or parsley
Salt, freshly ground pepper

SAUCE:
½ cup sour cream
½ cup mayonnaise
1 to 2 teaspoons fresh lemon juice
½ cup finely chopped fresh watercress or parsley
2 tablespoons chopped fresh mint
Salt, freshly ground white or black pepper

GARNISHES:
Fresh mint, watercress or parsley leaves

Halve the eggs lengthwise. Carefully remove the yolks and force them through a fine sieve. Mash in a shallow dish. Add mustard, mayonnaise, and watercress or parsley. Season with salt and pepper. Mix to blend well. Fill egg cavities with mixture, dividing equally, and press halves together neatly. Refrigerate, covered with plastic wrap, until ready to serve.

For the sauce. In a medium bowl combine the sour cream, mayonnaise, lemon juice, watercress or parsley, and mint. Season with salt and pepper. Refrigerate, covered with plastic wrap, 1 hour or longer to blend flavors.

To serve, arrange eggs on a serving dish. Spoon sauce over them, spreading evenly and decoratively. Garnish with fresh leaves. 6 servings.

# ❋ ISLAY OATEN CHEESE LOG

One of my favorite Scottish Western Islands is Islay (pronounced EYE-lay), the most southerly of the Inner Hebrides which has poignant reminders of its impressive past. The starkly beautiful High Cross of Kildaton is a masterpiece of stonecarving, and at Kilchoman there is a splendid medieval Celtic Cross. The Queen of the Hebrides, as it's aptly called, is also known for its unspoiled beauty, peaty Scotch malt whisky, goats' milk tablet, atmospheric pubs (notably the Lochside), fresh seafood, and Cheddar and Dunlop cheeses. Here's a starter made with the latter.

⅓ cup old-fashioned rolled oats
½ pound Dunlop or Cheddar cheese, shredded
½ cup (1 stick) unsalted butter, softened
2 teaspoons Worcestershire sauce
¼ teaspoon paprika
¼ teaspoon dry mustard
Freshly ground pepper

Spread oats in a medium ungreased skillet. Toast over medium-high heat, stirring 2 or 3 times, until edges are golden, about 3 minutes. Remove from heat; cool.

In a large bowl combine the shredded cheese, butter, Worcestershire, paprika, mustard, and pepper. Remove to a flat surface. Shape with the hands into a log or rectangle, about 7 inches long. Sprinkle with toasted oats to cover completely, pressing them into the log. Cover with plastic wrap. Refrigerate several hours, up to 3 days. Serve at room temperature with oatcakes or wheat crackers. Makes about 14 servings.

# ❀ EMERALD ISLE STUFFED MUSHROOMS

The magic of mushrooms can be readily appreciated when they are prepared as starters. Either raw or cooked, the mushrooms are tempting to the eye and tasteful to the palate. Although the most common of Ireland's many mushrooms is the field variety, cultivated ones are best for stuffing with various fillings. Some of them may be simple such as smoked oysters or herb-flavored cream cheese, or this ham combination. Stuffed mushrooms may be made ahead and kept in the refrigerator until ready to serve.

12 extra-large fresh mushrooms
About ½ cup (1 stick) unsalted butter
¼ cup minced scallions, with some pale green tops
1 clove garlic, peeled and crushed
1 tablespoon fresh lemon juice
½ cup finely chopped cooked ham
½ cup fine dry bread crumbs
½ teaspoon dried thyme
1 tablespoon chopped fresh parsley
Salt, freshly ground pepper

Preheat oven to 350 degrees.

Clean mushrooms by wiping with a damp cloth to remove any dirt. Pull out stems and mince. Brush caps with ¼ cup melted butter. Arrange in a shallow ovenproof dish, open sides up.

In a medium skillet melt ¼ cup butter over medium-low heat. Add scallions; sauté 1 minute. Stir in minced stems, garlic, and lemon juice. Sauté 3 minutes. Add ham, bread crumbs, thyme, and parsley. Season with salt and pepper. Mix well. Remove from stove. Spoon ham mixture into mushroom caps, dividing equally. Dot each one with a little butter. Bake in preheated oven until caps are tender, about 15 minutes. Serve hot. Makes 12.

# *Soups*

*View of Standing Stone, Skara Brae, Orkney Isles.*

*Sentiments about soup have long been emphatic. "Of*
*soup and love, the first is best.," wrote Thomas Fuller.*
*And, according to P. Morton Shand, "A woman who*
*cannot make soup should not be allowed to marry."*

The universal appeal of soups has been celebrated in lore, fable, literature, and verse. The famous French chef, Auguste Escoffier, wrote, "Soup puts the heart at ease, calms down the violence of hunger, eliminates the tensions of the day, and awakens and refines the appetite."

While travelling in Scotland and Ireland I always find a tempting variety of creative nourishing broths and soups. These specialties have long been basic and favorite fare, providing warmth, comfort, and good cheer as well as sustenance. They are also classically economical. Each of the countries has an appealing number of unique national favorites.

Dating back to Celtic times, soup-making has been an essential and laudable skill of the housewife who utilized the bounty of land and sea to make nourishing soups, flavored especially with herbs and vegetables. Many of them have not only innovative ingredients but fanciful names.

Over the years, as refinements in cooking improved, so did the preparation of creative soups enhanced with a wider selection of foods. But the lasting popularity of the old-fashioned soup is ample testimony to its goodness and appeal.

Soup is superb for every occasion. "Soup meals" are fun for suppers or informal dinners and can easily star at late evening parties. For the Gaels, soups have long been reliable friends, the mainstay at many tables through good and bad times. And, fortunately, homemade soups are still simmering in their kettles. Suffice it to say that soup *du jour*—of any day, any night and any meal—is a delight to prepare and enjoy.

# ❀ FARMHOUSE LEEK AND POTATO SOUP

Legend says that St. Patrick turned a clump of rushes into leeks which saved the life of a dying woman and established the leek as a favorite food.

Leeks, members of the onion family with sweet-flavored thick white bulbs, were treasured vegetables long before the arrival of New World potatoes in Gaelic lands. But eventually both became favorite staples, combined together in a number of national dishes, especially soups. Every cook has a favorite recipe for this one. Here's mine. Serve with ham slices and warm soda bread.

1 bunch (4 to 5) medium leeks
3 tablespoons unsalted butter
1 medium yellow onion, peeled and chopped
4 medium all-purpose potatoes, peeled and diced
3 cups vegetable or beef broth
½ teaspoon dried thyme
2 sprigs parsley
Salt, freshly ground pepper
3 cups hot milk or light cream
2 tablespoons chopped chives

Trim and discard dark green tops, tough outer leaves and roots of leeks. Halve white and light green parts lengthwise; wash under cold running water to remove all traces of soil. Slice cleaned leeks crosswise into thin strips.

In a large pot melt 2 tablespoons butter over medium-high heat. Add the leeks and onion. Sauté until translucent, about 5 minutes. Add potatoes, broth, thyme, and parsley. Season with salt and pepper. Bring to a boil. Reduce heat to medium-low.

Cover and cook slowly, stirring occasionally, until potatoes are tender, about 20 minutes. Take out and discard parsley sprigs. Add hot milk or cream and remaining 1 tablespoon of butter. Ladle soup into warm bowls. Serve garnished with chives. 6 to 8 servings. (Can be prepared 1 day ahead. Cool. Cover and refrigerate. Bring to a simmer before serving.)

## ❋ SKYE FISH CHOWDER

The mystical, rugged Isle of Skye off Scotland's northwestern coast is celebrated in song and legend. To cross "Over the Sea to Skye" is the thrill of a lifetime. For, in the words of H.V. Morton, "Skye stands alone, one of nature's supreme experiments in atmosphere." Like other visitors, I was enchanted with the topographically dramatic landscape and island's beauty. You are never more than five miles from the coast, and the sea figures in almost all aspects of daily living. Quite naturally there is an abundance of seafood to draw upon for chowders such as this one.

This is a good one-dish soup to serve with warm scones and slices of tomatoes and cheese for a weekend repast.

3 pounds mixed fish (cod, mackerel, haddock)
2½ quarts water
1 medium yellow onion, peeled and chopped
1 medium bay leaf
3 sprigs parsley
Salt, freshly ground pepper
2 tablespoons unsalted butter
1 large onion, peeled and sliced
3 medium all-purpose potatoes, peeled and quartered
1 cup sliced, scraped carrots
½ teaspoon dried thyme
1 cup spinach leaves, washed and stemmed
⅓ cup chopped fresh parsley

Have the fish cleaned and cut into fillets. Take home trimmings, heads and bones as well as fillets. Cut fillets into bite-size pieces. Put trimmings in a large pot. Add water, chopped onion, bay leaf, and parsley. Season with salt and pepper. Bring to a boil; skim. Lower the heat to medium-low. Cook slowly, uncovered, 20 minutes. Remove from heat; strain into a bowl. (Can be prepared 1 day ahead. Cool. Cover and refrigerate.)

Wash the pot. Add butter and melt over medium-high heat. Add sliced onion. Sauté until translucent, about 5 minutes. Add strained broth; bring to a boil. Reduce heat to medium-low. Add potatoes, carrots, thyme, and fish fillet pieces. Season with salt and pepper. Cook slowly, covered, until vegetables and fish are tender, about 20 minutes. Add spinach and parsley during last 5 minutes of cooking. Serve hot. 6 to 8 servings.

# ❀ BROTCHAN ROY

One of Ireland's oldest and most characteristic soups is made with three staple foods: leeks, oatmeal and milk. *Brotchan* is the Irish name for broth and the soup is also called *Brotchan Foltchep*, an old word for leek. The healthy dish is said to have been a favorite of St. Columba, the greatest Irish religious figure after Patrick. 'Tis a fitting dish for any occasion, but especially a holiday meal. Serve with warm soda bread and a cheese spread or slices of Blarney cheese.

1 bunch (4 to 5) medium leeks
2 tablespoons unsalted butter
4 tablespoons old-fashioned rolled oats
2 cups vegetable or beef broth
⅛ teaspoon freshly grated nutmeg
Salt, freshly ground pepper
2 cups light cream
2 tablespoons chopped fresh parsley or chives

Trim and discard dark green tops, tough outer leaves and roots of leeks. Halve white and light green parts lengthwise; wash under cold running water to remove all traces of soil. Slice cleaned leeks crosswise into thin strips.

In a large pot melt the butter over medium-high heat. Add oats; sauté until golden brown, about 3 minutes. Gradually add broth; bring to a boil, stirring constantly. Add sliced leeks and nutmeg. Season with salt and pepper. Reduce heat to medium-low. Cook slowly, uncovered, stirring occasionally, until thickened, about 30 minutes. Gradually add light cream. Leave over low heat until hot. Remove from heat; let stand 2 or 3 minutes. Serve garnished with parsley or chives. 6 servings. (Can be prepared 1 day ahead. Cool. Cover and refrigerate. Bring to a simmer before serving.)

# ❀ SCOTCH BROTH

The most traditional of all the Scottish soups is one called Barley Broth, Scots or Scotch Broth, a beloved combination of lamb, barley, and vegetables, which has given nourishment to Scots for centuries. It's one of those substantial dishes they call "Mouthful Soups" and is found in any pub or restaurant as a standard menu item in many variations. Here's one straight from the Highlands. Serve with warm bannocks or oatcakes.

2 pounds neck or breast of lamb, cut up
2 quarts water
Salt, freshly ground pepper
½ cup pearl barley
1 cup scraped diced carrots
1 cup peeled chopped onions
1 medium white turnip, peeled and diced
3 tablespoons chopped fresh parsley

Put lamb in a large pot. Add water. Season with salt and pepper. Bring to a boil over high heat; skim. Add the barley. Reduce heat to medium-low. Cover and cook slowly for 1½ hours. With tongs, remove lamb from pot. When cool enough to handle, cut meat from bones and trim any fat from it. Put meat back in the pot and discard the bones. Add carrots, onions, and turnip. Season with salt and pepper. Return to the stove. Bring to a boil. Reduce heat to medium-low. Cover and simmer until ingredients are tender, about 30 minutes. Stir in parsley before serving. 6 to 8 servings. (Optional ingredients are 2 cups shredded cabbage or shelled green peas.) (Can be prepared 2 days ahead. Cool. Cover and refrigerate. Bring to a simmer before serving).

# ❀ COUNTY CLARE WHITE ONION SOUP

The most widely cultivated and used of all vegetables, onions have long been treasured for their versatility and flavor in Gaelic lands. They have even had great medicinal power attributed to them, and have been used to treat an untold number of illnesses. In olden times this creamy comforting soup was taken by the Irish as a cure-all for a cold or other ailments. But, as my friend from County Clare advises, "'tis best to add a shot or two of good Irish whiskey, if ye really want to get well."

3 medium (about 1 pound) yellow onions
3 tablespoons unsalted butter
2 whole cloves
2 tablespoons all-purpose flour
3 cups chicken broth
⅛ teaspoon freshly grated nutmeg
1 medium bay leaf
1 cup light cream
Salt, freshly ground pepper

Peel onions and cut in quarters; slice thinly.

In a large pot melt butter over medium-high heat. Add sliced onions and cloves. Sauté until onions are translucent, about 5 minutes. Sprinkle with flour; mix well and cook, stirring, 1 minute. Gradually pour in broth, stirring as adding. Add nutmeg and bay leaf. Bring to a boil, stirring constantly. Lower heat to medium-low and cook slowly, covered, stirring occasionally, 30 minutes. Gradually add cream. Season with salt and pepper. Leave over low heat 5 minutes. Remove and discard cloves and bay leaf. 4 to 6 servings. (Can be prepared 2 days ahead. Cool. Cover and refrigerate. Bring to a simmer before serving.)

# ❀ DUNLOP CHEESE SOUP

Dunlop, a hard pressed cheese of the Cheddar variety is Scotland's best known, named after a town in the north of Ayrshire, where it was first made in 1688 by a dairy woman called Barbara Gilmour. A farmer's daughter, she had spent some time in Ireland. Upon returning to her native land she started making the cheese with milk from her cows, and within a few years it had become nationally known. In flavor it is mild and creamy with an appealing sharp aftertaste. A good soup for a luncheon entrée. Serve with buttered whole-wheat scones.

3 tablespoons unsalted butter
3 tablespoons finely chopped onions
3 tablespoons finely chopped scraped carrots
3 tablespoons all-purpose flour
4 cups chicken broth, preferably homemade
3 cups grated Dunlop or mild Cheddar cheese
1 cup light cream
¾ teaspoon dry mustard
⅛ teaspoon cayenne pepper
Salt, freshly ground pepper

In a large pot melt butter over medium-high heat. Add onions and carrots; sauté 6 minutes. Stir in flour; cook slowly 1 minute. Gradually add 1 cup chicken broth, stirring as adding. Then add remaining broth, still stirring as adding. Cook over medium-low heat 15 minutes. Remove from heat. Purée mixture in a food mill or food processor, with metal blade in place. Return to kettle. Slowly reheat. Gradually add cheese, stirring as adding, and continue to cook slowly until cheese is melted. (Can be prepared 1 day ahead. Cool. Cover and refrigerate. Bring to a simmer.) Stir in cream, mustard and cayenne pepper. Season with salt and pepper. Heat 4 minutes. Serve at once. 6 servings.

# ❀ YOUGHAL DILLED PRATIE SOUP

The potato or *pratie* is said to have been brought to Ireland from the New World in the late 16th century by Sir Walter Raleigh who planted the vegetable in the garden of his mansion, Myrtle Grove, in Youghal (pronounced "yawl"), now an attractive seaside town and fishing port east of Cork City. Ever since, the tubers flourished in the fertile soil and became an important staple of the Irish diet, cooked in every possible way, especially in soups. Serve this one with hot buttered oatcakes.

2 tablespoons unsalted butter
1 medium yellow onion, peeled and chopped
4 cups vegetable broth
3 cups diced, peeled potatoes (about 4 medium)
1 cup grated raw carrots
Salt, freshly ground pepper
2 cups light or sour cream
¼ cup chopped fresh dill or parsley

In a large saucepan melt butter over medium-high heat. Add chopped onion. Sauté until translucent, about 5 minutes. Pour in broth; bring to a boil over high heat. Add potatoes. Reduce heat to medium-low and cook, covered, until potatoes are tender, about 25 minutes. Stir in carrots. Season with salt and pepper. Add cream, dill or parsley. Leave on low heat for 5 minutes. 6 to 8 servings. (Can be prepared 2 days ahead. Cool. Cover and refrigerate. Bring to a simmer before serving.)

## ❀ ORKNEY LENTIL BRÖ

The extremely nutritious lentil, among the most ancient foods, was a Celtic favorite and is still used by the Gaels. This innovative soup is also called "red pottage" as it includes tomatoes and beets. The recipe is from the gently rolling Orkney Islands, collectively called Orkney and separated by a mere six miles from the northeastern tip of Scotland's mainland. It's a hearty soup for a winter supper. Serve with warm bannocks.

2 tablespoons unsalted butter
1 cup finely chopped onions
1 cup finely chopped scraped carrots
2 large ripe tomatoes, peeled, seeded and chopped
1½ cups brown lentils (about 10 ounces)
2 quarts water
½ teaspoon dried thyme
Salt, freshly ground pepper
1 cup diced, peeled cooked or canned beets
⅓ cup red wine vinegar

In a large pot melt butter over medium-high heat. Add onions and carrots. Sauté 6 minutes. Stir in tomatoes and cook 2 minutes. Add lentils, water, and thyme. Bring to a boil. Reduce heat to medium-low. Cook, covered, until lentils are tender, about 40 minutes. Season with salt and pepper. Add beets and vinegar. Cook another 5 minutes. 8 servings. (Can be prepared 3 days ahead. Cool. Cover and refrigerate. Bring to a simmer just before serving.)

# ❀ TIPPERARY MUSHROOM POTAGE

Wild mushrooms, members of the fungi family which are believed to have been the first plants to appear on earth, have long attracted people with a strange and compelling fascination. To the Celts they were mysterious and marvelous. Seeing them appear almost magically overnight, some persons believed that they were created by lightning bolts from heaven. Thus the strange foods were called "food of the Gods." In Ireland's County of Tipperary, mushrooms were once so plentiful that people recall how they seemed to spring right up out of the ground on hot August days. Now readily available cultivated mushrooms are used to make many dishes, including soups such as this one. It's a good first course soup for a weekend luncheon or supper.

⅓ cup unsalted butter
¾ cup chopped scallions, with some pale green tops
1 tablespoon fresh lemon juice
2 cups chopped, cleaned fresh cultivated mushrooms
4 cups strained vegetable or chicken broth
¾ cup chopped mixed fresh herbs (basil, chervil, dill, parsley)
Salt, freshly ground pepper

In a large saucepan melt butter over medium-high heat. Add scallions; sauté 2 minutes. Add lemon juice and mushrooms; sauté 4 minutes. Pour in broth; add herbs. Season with salt and pepper. Bring to a boil. Reduce heat to medium-low. Cook, covered, 25 minutes. 4 to 6 servings. (Can be prepared 2 days ahead. Cool. Cover and refrigerate. Bring to a simmer before serving.)

# ❀ COCK-A-LEEKIE

Although of Scottish origin, this famous chicken-and-leek soup is also an Irish favorite. Its name was acquired most probably because it was made with a cockerel or young rooster in the days when cock fighting was a popular sport and the defeated bird ended up in the soup pot. This is an easy modern recipe that is made with chicken breasts rather than a whole chicken. Serve with buttered warm scones for a holiday meal.

2 tablespoons unsalted butter
1 boneless skinless whole chicken breast, cut into thin strips
Salt and freshly ground pepper
4 medium leeks, white parts only, cleaned, sliced thin
6 cups chicken broth, preferably homemade
¼ cup long-grain rice
6 pitted prunes, cut into thin strips (optional)
¼ cup chopped fresh parsley

In a large saucepan melt butter over medium-high heat. Add chicken strips. Sauté until just cooked, about 5 minutes. Season with salt and pepper. With a slotted spoon, remove to a plate. Add leeks to drippings; sauté until soft, about 5 minutes. Pour in broth; bring to a boil. Stir in rice. Reduce heat to medium-low. Cook, covered, until rice is tender, about 20 minutes. Add sautéed chicken strips and prunes. Cook slowly another 5 minutes. Serve garnished with parsley. 8 servings. (Can be prepared 2 days ahead. Cool. Cover and refrigerate. Bring to a simmer before serving.)

*Kilkenny Castle.*

## ❀ DAME ALICE'S WITCH'S VEGETABLE SOUP

In Kilkenny City, called the medieval capital of Ireland, a fun place to dine is the Kyteler's Inn which dates back to 1324. It was once the home of Dame Alice Kyteler, a colorful character and alleged witch, accused of poisoning her four husbands. At the inn a "witch" greets guests with a glass of mulled wine and one may savor Irish specialties, including witch's broth, a hearty vegetable soup. This appealing variation is named for Dame Alice. Serve with ham and cheese sandwiches for a winter supper or pub party.

2 cups thinly sliced, peeled yellow onions
1 cup thinly sliced, scraped carrots
2 cups cauliflower florets
2 cups cut-up green beans
1 cup green peas
5 cups boiling water
1 tablespoon sugar
Salt, pepper to taste
6 tablespoons all-purpose flour
6 cups hot milk
2 tablespoons unsalted butter
⅓ cup chopped fresh dill or parsley

Put onions, carrots, cauliflower, green beans, and peas and boiling water in a large pot. Bring to a boil over high heat. Reduce heat to medium-low and cook slowly, covered, until vegetables are just tender, about 25 minutes.

In a medium bowl combine the flour and hot milk, whisk until smooth and thickened. Gradually stir into the hot soup; mix well. Continue to cook several minutes longer, until the liquid has thickened and vegetables are tender. Remove from heat. Add butter and dill or parsley. 8 to 10 servings. (Can be prepared 1 day ahead. Cool. Cover and refrigerate. Bring to a simmer before serving.)

# ❀ GIGHA CREAM OF SCALLOP SOUP

Scallops, bivalve mollusks highly prized for their delicate flavor and light, firm flesh, are a favorite Gaelic food. A small and sweet variety known as queen scallops are found in the Irish Sea and waters off Scotland's western coast. One delightful place to enjoy the seafood is Gigha (pronounced "Ghee-a" by the Gaels), a small southern Hebridean isle that has a rich historic past. Of all the island's gastronomic treats, I am particularly fond of the justly famous tiny sweet scallops, locally called clams. This flavorful cream soup is a superb first course for a special occasion dinner.

1 pound bay scallops
2 tablespoons unsalted butter
2 tablespoons finely chopped onions
3 tablespoons all-purpose flour
6 cups light cream or milk
2 teaspoons anchovy paste
2 to 3 teaspoons fresh lemon juice
Salt, freshly ground pepper
2 to 3 tablespoons finely chopped fresh dill or parsley

Remove any small particles from scallops. Rinse; drain, and dry. In a large saucepan melt butter over medium-high heat. Add onions. Sauté until translucent, about 5 minutes. Add flour. Cook, stirring, 3 minutes. Gradually add cream or milk, stirring as adding, and cook until slightly thickened and smooth, about 6 minutes. Stir in anchovy paste and lemon juice. Season with salt and pepper. Add scallops. Reduce heat to medium-low. Cook, covered, until scallops are just tender, about 4 minutes. Do not overcook or the scallops will be tough. Serve garnished with the dill or parsley. Serve at once. 6 servings

# Egg and Cheese Dishes

*B & B on Killrush main street.*

47

*In Scotland "Eggs were used in divining, the first laid-egg of a pullet being thought of as giving the best result when combined with fresh spring water. An egg white was dropped into a glass of water then a mouthful taken without swallowing. You then went for a walk and the first name that you heard spoken would be that of your future spouse."*

— *Scottish Customs*

Gaels treasure nourishing and innovative dishes starring two of man's earliest and most versatile foods—eggs and cheese, either separately or combined.

Gaelic folklore reveals that eggs and cheese have alluring, magical powers. One tale is that English witches always travelled on broomsticks; but the broomstick could not be used in Scotland for crossing lochs and rivers, and even for going from island to island in the sea. So an eggshell served as a boat. That's why Scottish boys and girls are taught to turn their eggshells upside down in the egg-cup, and to break them up with the spoon. They thus become useless to the witches.

Eggs, of course, are symbols of fertility and in the countryside were put in fields to ensure germination, upon which bountiful harvests depended. Eggs laid on Good Friday were believed never to go stale and were often preserved.

Cheeses were made for celebrations and many Scots give cheese as a prized New Year gift. A piece with a hole in it is thought to be particularly lucky. One belief in the Highlands was that if a traveller had lost his path on the misty moors, he could peer through the hole and find his way.

Gaels also looked to eggs as a chief source of nutrients. While most of our eggs now come from hens, those of geese, ducks, quail, and wild fowl as well as inland waterbirds provided important protein for Gaels when eaten fresh or preserved.

Particular delicacies were smoked eggs of solan geese, and roasted or lightly boiled tiny plovers' eggs.

Although eggs are important to all phases of cookery, as they are used in every type of dish, the basic methods for cooking them are limited. They are either boiled, baked, poached, scrambled, or fried. As such they have long played an important role in the Gaelic breakfast and remain the heart of it.

Omelets, soufflés, and other classic egg dishes, flavored according to local taste, and specialties made by combining eggs and cheese, are also favorite Scottish and Irish fare. In addition, Gaels enjoy a variety of cheese dishes made with the local products of each country. Some cheeses are eaten uncooked, either plain or with other foods, as common snacks and desserts.

Here is a representative collection of the best of egg and cheese delights that Scots and Irish have long enjoyed. A number of them can be made on the spur of the moment or hastily improvised. All are an important source of nutrition. While many are especially good for breakfasts and brunches, some of them may be served for other informal meals.

## ❀ DR. JOHNSON'S HIGHLAND EGGS

*"If an epicure could remove by a wish in quest of sensual gratifications, wherever he had supped, he would breakfast in Scotland,"* wrote Dr. Samuel Johnson, the irascible English critic of the Scots, after a visit in 1776.

The Scots have long enjoyed a hearty breakfast that lifts the spirits and gives energy and comfort. In fact, they have made their imaginative morning meal into an institution. Some persons even maintain that the best way to eat well in Scotland is to have breakfast three times a day. At any rate, all agree that it starts everyone in fine tune.

Standard items include baked eggs, often called farmhouse eggs, that are made in several variations. They are particularly good with shrimp, sautéed mushrooms, bits of cooked bacon, or simply cheese and cream. Here's one that I enjoyed in the Highlands where Dr. Johnson once travelled.

2 cups fresh whole-wheat bread cubes
1 cup grated Dunlop or sharp Cheddar cheese
8 thin slices bacon, cooked, drained, broken into pieces
4 eggs at room temperature
Freshly ground pepper
1 cup light cream
2 tablespoons chopped chives
Salt

Preheat oven to 350 degrees. Butter a 10-inch glass pie dish.

Sprinkle 1 cup bread cubes over bottom of prepared pie dish. Top with ½ cup grated cheese and half the bacon pieces. Carefully break eggs over ingredients, spacing evenly. Cover with remaining bread cubes, cheese, and bacon. Season with pepper to taste. Pour cream over ingredients. Bake in preheated oven until eggs are set, about 15 minutes. Sprinkle with chives. Season with salt. Serve at once. 4 servings.

# ❦ THE IRISH FRY

In Ireland the traditional Saturday night supper was a hearty Fry: a combination of potatoes, rashers or bacon, sausages, black and white puddings, and eggs, with the addition of fried bread, tomatoes, and mushrooms. It's still a popular meal but is commonly served as a bountiful breakfast that includes basic fry dishes plus fruit juice, cereals, brown bread, tea or coffee. It's what, as the Irish say, "should set you up for the day." Here's an attractive easy dish to serve for a weekend Fry.

## ❦ TOP O' THE MORNING POTATO-HAM OMELET

2 tablespoons unsalted butter
1 small yellow onion, peeled and minced
2 medium all-purpose potatoes, peeled and diced
1 cup diced cooked ham
½ cup minced green pepper
6 eggs at room temperature
¼ cup chopped fresh parsley
Salt, freshly ground pepper

Melt butter in a medium skillet over medium-high heat. Add minced onion; sauté until translucent, about 4 minutes. Stir in potatoes, ham, and green pepper. Cook, stirring often, until potatoes are fork tender, about 5 minutes.

Meanwhile, break eggs into a medium bowl; stir to blend well. Stir in parsley. Season with salt and pepper. Pour over potato-ham mixture. Cook, stirring occasionally, until eggs are set, about 4 minutes. Serve at once. 4 servings.

# ❀ COTTERED EGGS WITH SMOKED SALMON

Here's an easy dish to serve for a breakfast or brunch. Cottered is the Gaelic word for scrambled.

8 eggs at room temperature
2 tablespoons light cream
1 tablespoon chopped chives
2 teaspoons finely chopped fresh parsley
Salt, freshly ground pepper
4 tablespoons unsalted butter
1 cup diced smoked salmon
4 slices buttered whole-wheat toast

GARNISHES:
Chopped fresh dill or parsley, lemon wedges

Break eggs into a medium bowl. Add cream, chives, and parsley. Season with salt and pepper. Whisk to combine thoroughly. In a large skillet melt 3 tablespoons butter over medium-high heat. Pour in egg mixture. Reduce heat to medium-low and cook eggs, stirring, until almost set. Stir in diced salmon and remaining 1 tablespoon butter, cut into bits. Continue cooking until eggs are set but still moist and shiny, about 4 minutes. Serve over hot toast slices garnished with dill or parsley and lemon wedges, if desired. 4 servings.

# ❀ ADARE EGGS WITH SHRIMP

Adare, one of Ireland's prettiest villages, noted for its fine ecclesiastical ruins, thatched cottages, antique shops, and beautiful gardens is southwest of Limerick, not far from Shannon Airport. It's a great place for sightseeing and dining. Be sure to visit the Heritage Center which offers displays of the town's colorful history and has a fine café and craft shop. I've named this breakfast or brunch specialty for the attractive "Oh, sweet Adare!" that I enjoyed visiting on a fine June day.

6 hard-cooked eggs, peeled and chopped
½ pound (about 10) cooked & shelled large shrimp, diced
¾ cup light cream
1 tablespoon chopped fresh dill or parsley
2 teaspoons minced chervil
2 teaspoons Dijon-style mustard
½ cup grated Swiss-type cheese
Salt, freshly ground pepper
1 tablespoon unsalted butter, cut up

Preheat oven to 400 degrees. Butter a medium shallow baking dish.

In a medium bowl combine the eggs and shrimp. Add cream, dill or parsley, chervil, mustard, and ⅓ cup of cheese. Season with salt and pepper. Spoon into prepared dish. Sprinkle with remaining cheese; dot with butter. Bake in preheated oven until mixture is bubbly hot and golden on top, about 10 minutes. Serve at once. 4 servings.

# ❀ DRAPPIT EGGS

These "drappit-eggs," a colorful term for poached eggs, are an attractive breakfast or brunch dish.

4 slices hot buttered toast
4 teaspoons anchovy paste
4 hot poached eggs, drained
Salt, freshly ground pepper
8 small strips flat anchovies

Spread each slice of toast with anchovy paste. Arrange on individual plates. Top with a poached egg. Sprinkle with salt and pepper to taste. Arrange 2 strips anchovies crosswise on each egg. Serve at once with sausage patties, if desired. 4 servings.

# ❀ SCOTCH EGGS BENEDICT

Eggs Benedict, known as one of the "timeless classic egg dishes," is now prepared in many variations. This version, made with smoked salmon, a poached egg, and cheese sauce, is a winner.

2 English muffins, split, or 4 slices whole-wheat bread
8 thin slices smoked salmon, cut to fit over toast
4 hot poached eggs, drained
1 cup warm Cheese Sauce (recipe below)
Cayenne pepper

Toast English muffins or bread. Cover each muffin half or bread slice with 2 slices smoked salmon and a poached egg. Spoon ¼ cup Cheese Sauce (recipe below) over each egg. Sprinkle with a touch of cayenne. Serve at once. 4 servings.

CHEESE SAUCE:
2 tablespoons unsalted butter
2 tablespoons all-purpose flour
1 cup light cream
½ cup grated sharp Cheddar cheese
Salt, freshly ground pepper

In a small saucepan melt butter over medium-high heat. Stir in flour. Cook 1 minute. Gradually add cream and cook, stirring, until smooth and thickened, about 4 minutes. Stir in cheese. Cook 1 minute longer. Season with salt and pepper. Remove from heat. Makes 1 cup.

## ❊ WICKLOW PANCAKE

"Still south I went and west and south again,
    Through Wicklow from the morning till the night,
And far from cities, and the sites of men,
    Lived with the sunshine and the moon's delight."
                                    — John Synge, Prelude

Wicklow, aptly called the Garden of Ireland, stretching inland from the Irish Sea to the south, west, and north of Dublin, is a favorite holiday area, noted for its rolling granite hills, wild and desolate scenery, fine beaches, and country markets selling fresh produce, homemade jams and preserves, free-range chickens, and meaty sausages.

Although this traditional dish is called a pancake, it is actually a pancake-like omelet, made with eggs, bits of onion and potatoes, and herbs. Easy to make, simple to cook, and inexpensive, it can be eaten hot or cold and is great picnic fare.

3 to 4 tablespoons unsalted butter or vegetable oil
1 medium yellow onion, peeled and diced
1 large all-purpose potato, peeled and diced
Salt, freshly ground pepper to taste
4 eggs at room temperature
3 tablespoons chopped fresh parsley
4 teaspoons unsalted butter

In a medium skillet melt butter or heat oil over medium-high heat. Add diced onion and potato. Cook until onion is translucent and potato is soft, about 5 minutes. Season with salt and pepper.

Meanwhile, break eggs into a medium bowl. Add parsley. Season with salt and pepper. Pour half the egg mixture over the vegetables; tilt to spread evenly. Cook over medium-low heat, lifting up omelet around the edges to let wet mixture run underneath. Add remaining egg mixture and cook until golden brown and dry on top. Slide a spatula underneath to see if bottom is golden and to loosen. Remove from heat and invert a plate over omelet; turn over. Add more butter or oil to skillet. Return omelet to it. Cook until golden and crisp on other side. Serve cut into wedges with a pat of butter on each portion. Eat hot or cold. 2 servings.

# ❀ TRAMORE MUSHROOM-FILLED OMELET

Tramore, a short drive south from Waterford, has the air of an old-fashioned resort with a sandy beach, boardwalk, fairground, and Celtworld, an indoor attraction reflecting life in Ireland more than 1,500 years ago during Celtic times. Exhibits and animated displays recreate famous legends, myths, and folklore. A flavorful omelet made with some of the favorite Celtic foods is excellent for a brunch or lunch.

¼ cup (½ stick) unsalted butter
¼ cup chopped cleaned scallions, with some pale green tops
½ pound fresh mushrooms, cleaned and sliced thinly
3 tablespoons chopped fresh dill or parsley
⅛ teaspoon freshly grated nutmeg
Salt, freshly ground pepper
6 eggs at room temperature
3 tablespoons light cream or milk

In a medium skillet melt 2 tablespoons butter over medium-high heat. Add scallions; sauté 1 minute. Add mushrooms; sauté 4 minutes. Stir in dill or parsley and nutmeg. Season with salt and pepper. Keep warm.

Meanwhile, break eggs into a medium bowl. Stir to blend well. Add cream or milk. Season with salt and pepper. Melt remaining 2 tablespoons butter in an 8-inch skillet or omelet pan. Pour in egg mixture and tilt to spread evenly. Cook over medium-low heat until mixture begins to set. Loosen edges and tilt to let the wet mixture run underneath. When almost cooked on top but still a little moist, spoon some of the warm mushroom mixture onto one side. Fold over and slide onto a warm plate. Cover with remaining mushroom mixture. Serve at once. 4 servings.

# ❀ CHEESE-NUT FILLED POTATO PUFF

Here's an inexpensive cheese-nut filled mashed potato delight to serve as a vegetarian entrée or an accompaniment for meats or seafood. Prepare ahead and cook just prior to serving.

2 pounds (6 medium) all-purpose potatoes, peeled and cubed
Salt
9 tablespoons unsalted butter
Freshly ground pepper
5 small scallions, with some tops, cleaned and sliced
1 cup chopped walnuts
1 cup grated Cheddar cheese
Freshly grated nutmeg

Preheat oven to 375 degrees. Lightly butter a shallow round baking dish.

In a medium saucepan cook potato cubes in 2 inches lightly salted boiling water over medium-low heat until tender, about 12 minutes. Drain; return potatoes to low heat for a few seconds to remove all moisture. Turn potatoes into a large bowl. While still warm, mash with 4 tablespoons butter. Season with salt and pepper.

Meanwhile, in a small skillet melt 3 tablespoons butter over medium-high heat. Add scallions; sauté 2 minutes. Remove from heat. Set aside.

Spoon half the mashed potatoes, spreading evenly, into prepared dish. Sprinkle with chopped nuts, then scallions, and ½ cup cheese, spreading evenly. Cover with remaining half of mashed potatoes. Sprinkle the top with remaining ½ cup of cheese, 2 tablespoons melted butter, and a little nutmeg.

Bake in preheated oven until puffed and golden, about 35 minutes. To serve, cut into wedges. 4 to 6 servings.

## ❋ SCOTCH WOODCOCK

Some have said that this is one of the Scots' "cheap dishes," as it's made with scrambled eggs rather than woodcock, a favorite game bird. Perhaps a Scot did go hunting and returned home empty-handed, so his wife put together a creamy egg dish and called it "woodcock." But how this dish was given its name remains a mystery. Once served as a savoury, it's traditionally garnished with a pair of crossed anchovies that one Scot has said should be "crossed like the swords for a Highland sword dance, with only a pair of capers in each corner, symbolizing the dancer's heel and toe."

8 slices firm white bread
About 6 tablespoons unsalted butter
About 4 teaspoons anchovy paste
12 eggs, at room temperature
½ cup light cream
⅛ teaspoon cayenne pepper
Salt, freshly ground pepper
⅓ cup chopped fresh parsley (optional)

GARNISHES:
16 small strips flat anchovies
16 drained capers

Toast bread; spread each slice generously with butter and spread lightly with anchovy paste. Keep warm.

In a medium bowl combine the eggs, cream, and cayenne. Season with salt and pepper.

In a large skillet melt 3 tablespoons butter over medium-high heat. Add egg mixture. Cook, stirring frequently, until eggs are thickened but still moist and shiny, about 5 minutes. Mix in parsley. Spoon over warm toast, dividing evenly. Garnish with anchovies and capers. Serve at once. 6 to 8 servings.

## ✸ BACON-ONION-CHEESE TART

A savory tart made with bacon, onions, eggs, and cheese, is great to serve as a light main course, a first course, or part of a buffet spread. This one is easy to prepare and fun to serve.

6 slices thin bacon, cut into l-inch pieces
3 tablespoons unsalted butter
2 large yellow onions, peeled, cut in halves, sliced thinly
2 eggs at room temperature
½ cup heavy cream
1 teaspoon sugar
⅛ teaspoon freshly grated nutmeg
Salt, freshly ground pepper
1 9- or 10-inch pastry shell, baked
⅓ cup grated Cheddar cheese

Preheat oven to 375 degrees.

In a large skillet fry the bacon over medium-high heat until crisp; drain on paper towels; set aside. Remove all drippings except 1 tablespoon from skillet. Add butter; melt. Add onion slices. Sauté until translucent, about 7 minutes. Do not brown.

Break the eggs into a large bowl. Stir to blend well. Add the cream, sugar, and nutmeg. Season with salt and pepper. Mix again. Add sautéed onion slices; mix well. Spoon into pastry shell, spreading evenly. Sprinkle the top with grated cheese and cooked bacon pieces. Bake in preheated oven until filling is set in the center and is golden brown in spots, about 45 minutes. Remove from oven and cool on a wire rack. Serve warm or at room temperature, cut into wedges. 6 servings.

# ❀ SCOTCH RABBIT (RAREBIT)

There has been considerable gastronomical controversy concerning the proper name for this marvelous ale or beer-flavored cheese dish which dates back to the 18<sup>th</sup> century. Although not a reference to the animal, most culinary authorities maintain that the spelling of rabbit is correct but the dish is frequently and mistakingly referred to as "rarebit." Excellent for casual entertaining, the rabbit is ideally made at the table in a chafing dish and seasoned with Worcestershire sauce, mustard, and a touch of cayenne pepper.

As for the difference between a Welsh and Scotch rabbit, some say it's only that the Scots butter their toast and the Welsh do not.

2 tablespoons unsalted butter
1 pound sharp Cheddar cheese, coarsely grated
½ teaspoon dry mustard
1 teaspoon Worcestershire sauce
Dash cayenne pepper
Salt, freshly ground pepper
2 large egg yolks, beaten
½ cup light beer or ale
4 slices buttered toast

In a chafing dish or double boiler melt the butter. Add cheese and melt, stirring often in one direction. Add mustard, Worcestershire, and cayenne. Season with salt and pepper. Continue to stir in the same direction.

In a small dish combine egg yolks and beer or ale. Gradually add to cheese mixture, stirring as you do so. Cook over medium-low heat, never letting the mixture boil, and stirring almost continuously, until the mixture is smooth and velvety.

# Barley, Oats
# and
# Cornmeal

*Glorious midnight sunset, Outer Hebridean Isles.*

*"One curious tradition that persevered in Scotland well into the 20th century was based around oatmeal.*

*Scottish universities celebrated every February an annual holiday which was known as Mealy Monday. This was intended to give impoverished students the chance to return to their parents' home and restock the large bag of oatmeal that would then provide the basis for their meagre diet until the next year."*

— **Scottish Myths & Customs**

You will not find the name Loch Boisdale (Loch Baghasdail) on many maps. It's a quiet township and the main sea port on the twenty mile-long island of South Uist in Scotland's Outer Hebrides that was once a busy herring center and home of the clan MacDonald. And on a balmy June evening aboard a "CalMac' ferry I sailed from the picturesque port of Oban for this Loch to begin my tour of the remote Western Isles. I'd been booked by the Scottish Tourist Board to stay at a Bed and Breakfast and we arrived on schedule, past 1 A.M., after celebrating a glorious midnight sunset.

Waiting at the dock to greet me is my hospitable hostess with a welcoming message: "Get ye to bed for a little rest and we'll have the parritch ready in the morn." What a warm greeting—the promise of real Scottish porridge, one I'll never forget!

As the Scots say, all you need for a perfect porridge, besides the oats, is some fresh spring water, a little salt, and, ideally, Scottish hill or sea air. That next morning, I had it all. Except, that is, a Scottish dram or two of whisky, the proper Highland porridge adornment.

Edible seeds of the grass family, more commonly known as cereals or grains, have been man's most important food since prehistoric times. In Gaelic lands, barley and oats, and to a lesser extent, wheat and corn, provided necessary daily sustenance for the populace until modern times. Fortunately, inventive cooks utilized these foods in creating a good selection of dishes. Many are still treasured.

The history of civilization became intertwined with the quest for rich grain-bearing lands and the crops they yielded. It was the Celtic pursuit and development of new grains that laid down a stability in the areas where they settled. Even their diverse economy was based on cereal crops.

Since barley and oats were found to thrive in colder climates, they would become the cornerstone of the Gaelic diet, eaten especially as pottages and gruels, and made into breads. Until the introduction of oats, barley—one of the world's oldest food plants—was the predominant cereal of northern Celtic lands. It also supplied malt for brewing.

Oats, the most nutritious of grains and an excellent energy food, have sustained Gaels for centuries. They have a sweet, nutty flavor and crunchy texture and are an ideal cooking and baking ingredient. An old Scottish cookbook states quite correctly that the oat "is one of the sweetest grains to cook with." In several forms, they play an important role in Gaelic cuisines. Their cooks have created the most practical and imaginative of all the world's oat dishes.

Oats are a whole grain. Each hulled oat (or groat, as it is called) still contains its original bran, germ and endosperm. The most common form of oats, rolled oats, are so-called because the whole groats are steamed and then flattened between rollers before being made into flakes. The two most widely available in American stores are regular, or old-fashioned, and quick-cooking.

# ❀ PORRIDGE

'Tis claimed that porridge is a Celtic creation. Cuchulainn, the Irish Achilles, chosen hero of his people, whose life was a series of daring exploits and labors, had an inexhaustible appetite for porridge. The god Dagda was known as a sturdy porridge-eater. And Robbie Burns, the Scottish national bard, proclaimed, "The halesome parritch, Chief of Scotia's foods." There's an Irish saying that porridge puts roses in the cheeks and curls in the hair. For Gaels at home and abroad, porridge brings back many a fond memory as a beloved hot breakfast dish.

The celebrated Gaelic porridge developed over the years from a basic gruel or brose, made originally with bere, or barley meal, and then more often with oatmeal, into a traditional creation with a personality of its own. The word porridge is now associated with oatmeal, made and served with fascinating tradition and ritual.

For porridge, the Scots and Irish use milled (a more coarsely ground product) rather than rolled oats. The latter produce a creamy, smooth porridge and milled oats make a coarser and crunchier mixture. Old-time recipes stipulate that the dish should be simmered gently and mention the importance of "swelling the meal." Salt is an essential ingredient as it brings out the flavor of the oats.

Once the milk for the morning parritch came straight from the cow and the cooked mixture was flavored only with a pinch or two of salt. But most Gaels now prefer a sweetener—a spoonful of honey, golden syrup or brown sugar. Sprinkling white sugar over porridge is frowned upon by purists.

Porridge need not always be the same traditional dish. Enhance it with some currants or raisins, chopped nuts, thinly sliced dried fruit, or a dash of ground cinnamon or nutmeg. For toppings, sprinkle with toasted oats, sliced fresh fruit, or berries in season.

Porridge by tradition is spoken of, respectfully, as "they." ". . . they're grand food, parritch," wrote Robert Louis Stevenson in *Kidnapped*.

## ✸ STIRABOUT

In Scotland and Ireland porridge was once called stirabout, because it was stirred in a clockwise direction (following the course of the sun) with the right hand. Gaels believe this routine ensures good luck. To eat properly, ladle the mixture into individual bowls or porringers, and then dip each spoonful into a a side dish of cold cream or milk, giving a desirable contrast of hot and cold as it is eaten.

Old Celtic laws stipulated the type of stirabout and its flavoring that children should eat. Those of workmen were to have oatmeal stirabout made with buttermilk or water. Sons of chieftains rated a dish enhanced with fresh milk and fresh butter. Whereas, the sons of kings dined on wheaten stirabout served with new milk and honey.

Here's a basic stirabout or porridge recipe for everyone.

2 cups water
1 cup Scottish-style porridge oats
Salt to taste

In a medium saucepan bring the water to a boil over medium-high heat. Gradually add oats, stirring with a wooden spoon. Reduce the heat to medium-low. Cook, uncovered, stirring frequently, until oats are softened and very thick, about 5 minutes. Season with salt. Serve hot with cream or milk, adding sugar or another sweetener to taste. Top with chopped dried or fresh fruit, if desired. 4 servings.

# ❀ RAISIN-WALNUT PORRIDGE

This is a good change-of-pace porridge for a company breakfast.

½ cup chopped walnuts
3 cups water
½ cup raisins
1⅓ cups old-fashioned rolled oats
Salt
2 tablespoons unsalted butter
4 tablespoons light brown sugar
4 tablespoons light cream or milk

In a small skillet sauté chopped walnuts over medium heat until lightly toasted, about 3 minutes. Remove from heat; set aside.

In a medium saucepan bring the water to a boil over medium-high heat. Stir in raisins. Reduce heat to medium-low and simmer until raisins are plumped, about 3 minutes. Return liquid to a boil. Gradually add oats, stirring with a wooden spoon. Cook, uncovered, stirring frequently, until oats are softened and very thick, about 5 minutes. Season with salt. Stir in butter and toasted walnuts. Serve hot sprinkled with brown sugar and with cream or milk. 4 servings.

# ❀ GIANT MacASKILL'S OATMEAL BROSE

When I was a child my mother often spoke about her famous cousin, a giant named Angus MacAskill, once "the strongest man on earth." Although she had not met her hero, she knew all about the seven-foot, nine-inch 450-pound man who was born on the Scottish Island of Berneray in the Outer Hebrides. When Angus was six years old the MacAskill family migrated to Canada and settled on Cape Breton Island, the beloved homeland of my parents.

As Angus grew into manhood, stories about his strength and Bunyanesque feats reached the American showman, P.T. Barnum, who took the Scotsman on tour in the mid 1800s, billing him with Tom Thumb as the world's largest and smallest human beings.

In the small fishing village of Saint Ann's, Cape Breton, there is a Giant MacAskill-Highland Pioneer's Museum, dedicated to his memory. And, at Dunvegan on the Island of Skye, there's another museum that records his life and times. Although I was not able to find out much about the giant's daily fare, he was, just like all the "braw Scotch laddies" brought up on a diet of oatmeal dishes, especially parritch.

Oatmeal brose is different from porridge as it's made by pouring boiling water over meal, sort of an instant cereal. Here's a modern recipe for an ancient dish.

1 cup old-fashioned rolled oats
1 cup hot milk
Salt
1 tablespoon unsalted butter
1 tablespoon golden raisins or chopped apricots

70

Put oats in a small bowl. Add the hot milk, stirring while adding. Season with salt. Stir in butter and raisins or apricots. Serve at once. 1 serving.

*Giant MacAskill Museum.*

# ✿ IRISH PINHEAD OATMEAL

The cool, moist climate and fertile soil of Ireland produce exceptional milling oats. The best known of the Irish oatmeals is McCanns. In 1800, John McCann founded his mills at Beamond, on the edge of the Nanny River, and began exporting oatmeal to the United States in 1871. McCann's steel cut, or pinhead, Irish Oatmeal are sold throughout the country in a unique white, black and gold printed tin. With steel-cut oats, the groats are cut into pieces between steel rollers, making for a textured cereal. The term pinhead describes what the oat looks like once it has been cut by steel blades into small, round, pearly nuggets.

¼ cup coarsely chopped walnuts
1 tablespoon honey
4 cups cold water
1 cup Irish pinhead oatmeal, such as McCann's
Salt
¼ cup raisins
¼ cup brown sugar
½ teaspoon ground cinnamon
Heavy or light cream

In a small skillet sauté chopped walnuts over medium heat until lightly toasted, about 3 minutes. Drizzle honey over them, stirring to coat well. Remove skillet from heat. Take out walnuts and let cool.

In a medium heavy saucepan bring the water to a boil over high heat. Gradually add oatmeal, stirring with a wooden spoon. Reduce heat to medium-low and cook, uncovered, stirring often, until oats are softened and very thick, about 30 minutes. Season with salt. Stir in raisins, brown sugar, and cinnamon. Serve porridge in small bowls topped with the honey walnuts, dividing evenly, and with cream. 4 servings.

# ❊ KIRKWALL BARLEY PORRIDGE

Barley porridge was once a staple breakfast dish in the Scottish Highlands and Islands. It was made with a rare and ancient variety of barley called *bere* (pronounced bare), important for malting and bread making. Now grown only on Scotland's Orkney Islands, the high fiber meal is used primarily for making nutty-flavored bannocks, and is mixed with flour for scones. In Kirkwall, the capital and an ancient trading crossroads lying on a beautiful landlocked bay, I enjoyed a hearty barley porridge that can be made in America with whole hulled barley, also called hulled barley and Scotch barley. Sold in specialty food stores, this brown barley is nuttier and chewier than pearl barley.

2½ cups cold water
Salt
1 cup hulled barley
1 tablespoon unsalted butter
½ cup golden or maple syrup
¼ cup light cream

In a medium heavy saucepan bring the water to a boil over high heat. Gradually add barley, stirring as adding. Reduce heat to medium-low. Cook, covered, stirring occasionally, until barley is tender but chewy, about 1 hour. Check for doneness during cooking. Remove from heat. Stir in butter. Serve with the syrup and cream, mixed together. 4 servings.

# ❀ BARLEY-MUSHROOM CASSEROLE

This is a superb accompaniment for meat or poultry.

6 tablespoons unsalted butter
1 large yellow onion, peeled and chopped
8 ounces or 3 cups sliced, cleaned mushrooms
1 tablespoon fresh lemon juice
1 cup pearl barley
1 teaspoon dried tarragon
3 cups hot chicken broth
Salt, freshly ground pepper
⅓ cup chopped fresh dill or parsley

Preheat oven to 375 degrees. Butter a 2-quart baking dish.

In a large heavy saucepan melt butter over medium-high heat. Add chopped onion; sauté until translucent, about 5 minutes. Add mushrooms and lemon juice; sauté 4 minutes. Stir in barley and tarragon; sauté 1 minute. Pour in hot chicken broth. Season with salt and pepper. Slowly bring to a boil. Remove from heat and turn into prepared dish. Cover and bake in preheated oven until barley is tender, about 55 minutes. Remove from stove; stir in dill or parsley. Serve hot. 6 to 8 servings.

# ❀ FRUMENTY

In olden days a pottage called a frumenty or furmenty was a simple concoction of boiled wheat or oatmeal mixed with milk and perhaps spices, sometimes enjoyed as a harvest celebration dish. Over the years it evolved into a sweet pudding flavored with honey, spices, and nuts. Here's a dressed-up version enhanced with pears, raisins, walnuts, and spices to serve as a breakfast or brunch accompaniment or a dessert, if desired.

2 tablespoons unsalted butter
2 cups light cream or milk
3 tablespoons honey
¼ teaspoon salt
1 cup old-fashioned rolled oats
3 eggs, at room temperature, separated
2 medium ripe firm pears, pared, cored, and diced
½ cup golden raisins
½ cup chopped walnuts
¼ teaspoon each of ground cloves, nutmeg, and cinnamon

Preheat oven to 350 degrees. Butter a 1½-quart baking dish.

In a medium heavy saucepan combine the butter, cream or milk, honey, and salt. Bring just to a boil over high heat. Gradually add oats, stirring constantly with a wooden spoon. Lower the heat to medium. Cook, uncovered, stirring occasionally, until softened and very thick, about 5 minutes. Remove from heat; cover. Let stand 3 minutes, or until of desired consistency. Spoon into a large bowl.

In a small dish mix egg yolks slightly with a fork. Add to oat mixture, mixing thoroughly. Stir in diced pears, raisins, walnuts, cloves, nutmeg, and cinnamon.

In another large bowl beat egg whites until stiff. Fold gently into oat mixture. Spoon into prepared baking dish. Bake in preheated oven until pudding is set and cooked, about 45 minutes. Serve at once with cream or milk, if desired. 4 to 6 servings.

# ❀ SCOTTISH MUËSLI

In modern times Scots have been devotees of cold "natural" cereals that have a lot of nutrients. *Muësli* and other marvelous mixtures of uncooked oats, fruit, nuts, milk, and sometimes other foods, are sophisticated versions of the ancient Scottish *brose*.

2 cups rolled old-fashioned oats
¼ cup oat bran
1¼ cups cold low fat milk
1 large unpeeled red apple, cored and finely chopped
1 to 2 teaspoons fresh lemon juice
¾ cup golden raisins
⅓ cup chopped blanched almonds
3 to 4 tablespoons honey, preferably heather

Place oats and oat bran in a medium bowl; add milk. Let stand at room temperature 45 to 60 minutes. Add chopped apple and lemon juice; mix well. Stir in raisins, almonds, and honey; mix well. Refrigerate 2 to 3 hours before serving. Serve with a few banana slices, if desired. 4 servings.

# ✻ HASTY PUDDING

Gaelic lore says that hasty pudding was concocted when housewives used everyday staples such as flour or oatmeal, milk, and flavorings to make a pleasing dish in a short time for unexpected guests. Over the years other foods were added to the basic ingredients but, essentially, the pudding remained a simple supper specialty, sometimes served with a sauce or gravy. When yellow corn meal or "maize" was originally imported into Ireland from America during the famine of the 1850s, it too was used to make hasty puddings. Apples, ginger, brown sugar, and molasses give a new flavor to an old favorite.

1½ cups cold water
1 cup yellow cornmeal
¾ teaspoon salt
1 teaspoon ground ginger
2 cups milk
1 large tart apple, peeled, cored and diced
⅓ cup light brown sugar
¼ cup light molasses or golden syrup

In a large heavy saucepan combine the water, cornmeal, and salt over medium-low heat. Cook, stirring frequently, until mixture thickens, about 6 minutes. Stir in the ginger. Gradually add the milk and diced apple, stirring as adding, until mixture comes to a boil. Continue cooking over medium-high heat, stirring frequently, until mixture is thick and smooth, about 10 minutes. Stir in the sugar and molasses or syrup during the last 5 minutes of cooking. Remove from stove. Let stand, covered, 20 minutes. Serve in bowls with cream, if desired. 6 servings.

# ❋ CORNMEAL WITH CHEESE

Here's a good accompaniment for meat or poultry.

1 cup yellow cornmeal
1 cup cold water
1 teaspoon salt
3 cups boiling water
1 cup farmer's or cottage cheese, drained and crumbled
1 cup grated Swiss-type cheese
1 cup herb-flavored tomato sauce
2 tablespoons fine dry breadcrumbs
1 tablespoon unsalted butter, melted

Preheat oven to 350 degrees. Butter a 1½-quart baking dish.
In a medium bowl combine the cornmeal, 1 cup cold water, and salt. Mix vigorously to form a thick paste. Turn cornmeal paste all at once into boiling water in a large heavy saucepan. With water still boiling, stir constantly with a wooden spoon to keep the mixture smooth. Reduce the heat to medium-low and cook, covered, until cornmeal is very thick, about 10 minutes.

Remove from the heat and spoon ⅓ of the cornmeal mixture into prepared casserole. Top with ⅓ cup farmer's or cottage cheese, ⅓ cup grated cheese, and ⅓ cup tomato sauce. Repeat the layers. Sprinkle top with breadcrumbs and melted butter. Bake in preheated oven until hot, bubbly and golden on top, about 30 minutes. Serve warm. 6 servings.

# ❀ SKIRL-IN-THE-PAN

Skirlie or skirl-in-the-pan is an old Scots dish made from oatmeal, suet, and onions, that was served with mashed potatoes and a glass of cold buttermilk for a nourishing supper. Versatile and noted for its appealing nutty texture, the mixture can be served on its own or as an accompaniment; used as a stuffing for poultry, game or vegetables; cooked like dumplings and simmered in soups or stews; or made into a pudding. The name comes from the noise the suet makes while cooking in the pan which might suggest skirling of bagpipes.

¼ cup (½ stick) unsalted butter
2 medium yellow onions, peeled and finely chopped
1½ cups rolled oats
⅓ cup chopped fresh parsley
Salt, freshly ground pepper

In a medium heavy saucepan melt butter over medium-high heat. Add chopped onions; sauté until translucent, about 5 minutes. Stir in oats and cook, stirring often, until the butter is absorbed by the oats, about 10 minutes. The mixture should be fairly dry. Stir in parsley. Season with salt and pepper. Serve on buttered toast, if desired. Or use as suggested above. Makes about 2½ cups.

# Seafood

*Lobster pots, Crail Harbor, Scotland.*

> "Aphrodite was born of the sea, and was commonly
> held to exercise her influence through certain products
> of the sea, notably (in the Scottish tradition) trout,
> skate, shell-fish and salt. Skate-bree (the liquor in
> which skate has been boiled) is a famous old Scottish
> love-potion."
>
> — *The Scots Kitchen*

Of all the Gaelic gastronomic delights, none is more fascinating and pleasurable than the superb seafood. One can envisage the colorful fishing vessels heading out to the ocean or one of the surrounding seas in early morn and returning later with the day's catch. The fish markets burst forth with excitement amid the din of loud and anxious bargaining. And then the eating! Nothing can compare with the fresh flavor of each fish or crustacean whether served in a rustic pub, a seaside restaurant, or in the home.

While travelling in Scotland and Ireland one is constantly lured to the table by seafood temptations. For both are countries of fish and shellfish, blessed with hundreds of miles of twisting coastline, islands, fine sea-lochs, and freshwater streams that yield a varied and bountiful harvest. Little wonder that seafood has long been staple fare and that the cooks developed an inviting repertoire of nourishing dishes featuring them.

In Celtic times fishing was a common pursuit and seafood provided a valuable addition to the diet. Commonly cooked on spits over open fires in areas where they were found, salmon was the most prized of all fish but trout, sea fish, and shellfish also were eaten.

For generations, the Scots and Irish have excelled in the art of curing fish by drying, salting and smoking them. With methods introduced by the Vikings, they relied mainly on the use of the elements (sun-dried or wind-dried) to give the fish more flavor.

Among the innovative specialties, the most famous and beloved is kippers, or kippered herring, which have a distinctive subtle taste and are revered as a culinary prize by Gaels around the world.

From early times to the present day, the small, bony, humble salt herring, caught in great quantities in the North Sea and Atlantic, formed, along with oatmeal, the backbone of the Gaelic diet. So important were the fish, valued for their high protein and low cost, that countries fought over them. "It's nae fish ye're buying, it's men's lives." wrote Sir Walter Scott.

Because fresh herring deteriorate rapidly, salting down the fish was once the best way to keep them for export and store for year-round use. Their strong flavor was said to ward off hunger and it enhanced bland foods.

Another highly prized specialty is Findon or finnan haddock, better known as finnan haddie, a pale golden delicacy with soft tender flesh and a mild but assertive smoky flavor. The name comes from Findon, one of the windswept villages along Scotland's northeastern coast where the fisherfolk originated the now-famous method of smoking the fish over a peat fire.

Sold whole or in fillets, the firm, white fish lends itself to a variety of inviting dishes, from fish cakes to kedgeree, and is served as a classic breakfast dish, first course and entrée in Scotland's and Ireland's dining places.

Unless salted or otherwise preserved, fish has been enjoyed only in season. Since the natural flavor of each fresh or salt water denizen should be preserved, seafood in Gaelic lands is prepared simply, and with foods that enhance it.

With this collection of recipes, one can readily comprehend the appeal of the marvelous marine delicacies.

# ❀ KING OF FISH: THE SALMON OF KNOWLEDGE

*"To what meals the woods invite me/ All about!/
There are water, herbs and cresses, Salmon, trout."*
*The Hermit's Song: 7ᵗʰ Century*

"The King Fish," salmon, taken from the Atlantic and famous Scottish and Irish rivers, has always been relished for its delicate flesh and superb flavor. While early Gaels enjoyed pickled and spiced salmon, the simplest methods of cooking are best: boiling, steaming, baking and grilling. There is no equal to poached fresh salmon, cooked gently in salted water, and served with lemon juice and butter or a flavorful sauce. This is truly a pleasurable repast, one of the world's greatest treats.

Salmon has figured in legend since ancient times and there are many fascinating tales about it. According to Irish mythology, there was only one creature wiser than man: the fabled Salmon of Knowledge which had fed upon the acorns of the Tree of Knowledge. It was said that whoever tasted of the salmon would inherit its wisdom and foresight.

After devoting several years to capturing the prized fish, an old soothsayer finally accomplished his goal. But he assigned the cooking of the salmon to his young servant, with a warning not to taste it. Alas, during the cooking, the boy burned his finger and, to relieve the pain, stuck the finger in his mouth. Thus, he became the first person to taste the Salmon of Knowledge and to acquire its magical powers. The lad later became the great Irish warrior hero, Fionn McCumhaill or Finn MacCool, who devoted the rest of his life to extolling wisdom.

Here are three salmon recipes.

# ❀ DUNGUAIRE CASTLE POTTED SALMON

Kinvara is a charming fishing village on the southwest corner of Galway Bay known for its boats' festival and the nearby majestic Dunguaire Castle which has, for hundreds of years, stood on the site of the 7th century stronghold of Guaire, the king of Connaught. Today the restored castle welcomes guests to its summer Medieval Banquets that honor local writers and others with ties to western Ireland, including the celebrated poet, William Butler Yeats and his friend, Lady Gregory.

Potted salmon is an old traditional dish, once served for breakfast and high tea. Now it makes a marvelous pub, buffet or picnic specialty. Simple to prepare, the dish can be kept ready in the refrigerator for unexpected guests on any occasion. Here's one tasty easy recipe.

6 tablespoons (¾ stick) unsalted butter, softened
1½ cups minced cooked salmon, skinned and boned
2 tablespoons minced scallions
1 tablespoon fresh lemon juice
1 teaspoon Worcestershire sauce
Freshly ground pepper

In a large bowl beat the softened butter and minced salmon to make a smooth paste. Mix in the scallions, lemon juice, Worcestershire, and pepper. Spoon mixture into 1 or 2 pots, bowls or molds. Cover with plastic wrap. Refrigerate several hours, up to 4 days. Leave at room temperature about 1 hour before serving. Garnish with a leaf of watercress or parsley, if desired. Serve with thin slices of brown bread. Makes 1½ cups.

# ❀ CONNEMARA BAKED SALMON STEAKS

Connemara is a land of enthralling rugged beauty, wild and haunting terrain, and pond-studded bogs on the west coast of Ireland. Here myth and legend are an integral part of the Celtic search for what the famed Irish poet Yeats called "the infinite things the world has never seen." It's also known for salmon fishing. Driving in The *gaeltacht*—Irish speaking—region along winding roads through fishing villages and market towns is a wondrous experience. Here also is the beautiful Ballynahinch River where some of the world's best salmon can be observed leaping, displaying their beauty to delighted spectators, before they are caught. Here's an inviting way of preparing salmon steaks.

3 tablespoons fresh lemon juice
2 tablespoons olive oil
1 tablespoon honey
6 salmon steaks, about 1-inch thick
Salt, freshly ground pepper
3 tablespoons unsalted butter, cut up
2 large yellow onions, peeled and sliced thinly
¾ cup dry white wine
½ cup chopped fresh dill or parsley

Preheat oven to 400 degrees. Butter a large shallow baking dish.

In a small dish, combine the lemon juice, olive oil, and honey. Pat steaks dry. Brush with lemon-oil mixture. Season with salt and pepper.

Meanwhile, melt butter in a medium skillet over medium-high heat. Add onions; sauté until translucent, about 5 minutes. Spoon into prepared baking dish. Top with salmon steaks. Sprinkle with wine. Bake, covered, in preheated oven, until salmon separates easily with a fork and is no longer translucent, about 25 minutes. Remove salmon to a platter; top with onions and pan juices. Garnish with dill or parsley. Serve at once. 6 servings.

## ❀ DILL SALMON

Cured dill-flavored salmon called *gravlax* is now a treasured Northern Scottish specialty that originated in Scandinavia. It may be eaten as a main course, a buffet dish, or as a starter with brown bread or oatcakes.

1 large bunch fresh dill, cleaned
2 pounds center-cut fresh salmon fillets, skin left on
¼ cup coarse salt
¼ cup sugar
3 teaspoons crushed white peppercorns

Coarsely chop the dill, reserving some of the sprigs for a garnish. Remove any small bones from the salmon. In a small dish combine the salt, sugar, and pepper. Rub half of this mixture over both sides of the salmon. Place the salmon, skin side down, in a nonreactive baking dish. Sprinkle the top with the rest of the mixture. Place the chopped dill over it. Cover the dish with plastic wrap and then aluminum foil. Top with a heavy dish to weight it down. Refrigerate for 24 hours, turning once or twice during this period.

To serve, remove salmon from the dish and scrape off marinade and dill. Cut off the skin; slice diagonally into thin slices. Serve slices garnished with fresh dill. 4 to 6 servings.

Here are some other seafood recipes.

## ❀ DUBLIN LAWYER

This Irish traditional dish, made with a live lobster split in half, is called Dublin Lawyer or Drunken Lobster as the flesh is flambéed in Irish whiskey. Serve for a dinner for two.

1 fresh lobster, about 2 pounds
½ cup (1 stick) unsalted butter, cut up
Salt, freshly ground pepper
½ cup Irish whiskey
½ cup light cream

Cook the lobster in a pot of salted boiling water. Take out of the water; halve lengthwise. Remove meat from tail and claws. Cut into bite-size pieces. Keep the lobster shell halves.

In a medium skillet melt the butter over medium-high heat. Add the lobster pieces. Sauté 1 or 2 minutes to coat well with butter. Season with salt and pepper. Pour in whiskey and when heated, ignite it. When flame dies, stir in the cream. Leave on the stove long enough to heat it. Remove lobster from skillet and spoon into reserved shells. Serve in the shells. 2 servings.

## ❀ ULLAPOOL HERBED FISH CAKES

The little town of Ullapool in Scotland's northwestern Webster Ross region, custom-built as a herring station in the 1780s, is a busy picturesque port with well-built stone cottages and pleasant lodgings serving locally caught seafood. It's also the embarkation point for trawlers crossing the Minch, a section of the North Atlantic separating the mainland from the Outer Hebrides, and the car-ferry to Stornaway on the Island of Lewis.

Fish cakes, made with either fresh or smoked seafood, are always a good choice for an informal meal. Here's one of my favorite recipes for them.

2 cups (1 pound) flaked cooked cod or haddock
2 cups hot seasoned, freshly mashed potatoes
3 eggs
6 tablespoons unsalted butter, softened
3 tablespoons minced scallions
½ teaspoon dried thyme
3 tablespoons chopped fresh herbs (dill, tarragon, parsley)
Salt, freshly ground pepper
About 1 cup fine dry bread crumbs

In a large bowl combine the cooked fish, mashed potatoes, 1 egg, 2 tablespoons butter, scallions, thyme, herbs, and pepper. Mix well. With floured hands, shape into 8 balls; flatten them into round shapes. Put 2 eggs, beaten, and bread crumbs in separate shallow dishes. Coat each cake first with beaten egg and then with crumbs, patting them evenly on both sides. Place on a plate. Refrigerate, covered with plastic wrap, up to 8 hours, until 20 minutes before frying.

Melt 4 tablespoons butter in a large skillet over medium-high heat. Add the fish cakes, several at a time, and fry until golden brown on each side, turning once, about 10 minutes. Serve at once with lemon wedges. 8 servings.

# ✿ BARRA TROUT FRIED IN OATMEAL

Barra, at the southern end of the Outer Hebrides, is a beautiful island with an astonishing range of wild flowers and a variety of scenery, from grassy *machairs* (seaside sandy tracts) to rocky shores. Legend says the isle was named after St. Finnbarr, a missionary of the old Celtic Church who came there from Iona. For centuries Barra has been associated with the Clan MacNeil, once famed as notorious pirates, and the major attraction is Kisimul Castle, the clan's stronghold, dating from the 13th century.

The Isle of Barra Hotel is known for its atmospheric pub, renowned as the most westerly in Scotland, where one can have "the last dram before America." The fine fare here and in other island dining places features seafood, including the sweet, small, speckled brown trout which are found in the local waters.

Wash and dry a cleaned trout, allowing 1 per person. Dip each one in milk and dredge on both sides with oatmeal. Season with salt and pepper. To cook, fry in heated oil or butter or bacon fat in a large skillet over medium-high heat until golden on both sides and the flesh is fork tender. Serve at once topped with a cube of butter and lemon wedge.

## ❋ SKIBBEREEN SCALLOP-MUSHROOM PIE

Described by one writer as "a cheerful Irish jig of a place," Skibbereen is the main market town in southwest Cork and has many bright-painted houses and fine places for eating seafood. While dining here or in other Irish seacoast locales it's always a delight to find scallops which are wrapped in bacon and broiled or fried, served in creamed dishes, or in pies like this one.

½ pound sea scallops, rinsed and drained
¾ cup milk
4 tablespoons unsalted butter
¼ pound fresh mushrooms, cleaned and sliced
2 tablespoons all-purpose flour
¼ cup dry sherry or cider
2 cups hot seasoned, freshly mashed potatoes
Chopped fresh dill or parsley

Preheat broiler. Butter a 9-inch glass pie plate.

In a medium saucepan combine the scallops and milk. Bring to a boil over high heat. Reduce the heat to low and simmer 5 minutes. Drain, reserving the milk. Cut the scallops in half.

In a medium saucepan melt 2 tablespoons butter. Add mushrooms; sauté until just tender, 3 to 4 minutes. Stir in the flour. Gradually add the reserved milk. Bring to a boil, stirring constantly, over high heat until the sauce thickens. Reduce heat. Simmer 3 or 4 minutes. Add the scallops. Stir in the sherry or cider. Leave on medium-high heat 2 minutes. Spoon into prepared pie plate. Cover ingredients with mashed potatoes, spreading evenly. Sprinkle the top with the remaining 2 tablespoons butter, melted.

Place under preheated broiler, 4 inches from heat. Broil until bubbly hot and top is golden brown, about 3 minutes. Serve immediately, garnished with chopped dill or parsley. 4 servings. (The dish can be made partially beforehand and broiled just before serving.)

## ✿ OBAN BAKED COD WITH VEGETABLES

Like hundreds of other travellers, I've whiled away many enjoyable hours waiting for a ferry to the Hebridean Islands in the bustling port and resort town of Oban, "small bay," in Argyll on the Firth of Lorne. Once a prominent fishing center and Mac-Dougall stronghold and now an important tourism center, Oban is a lively Gaelic town where summer Pipe Band concerts and September Highland Games are held. The town also has inviting dining places that serve local mussels, Loch Fyne kippers, smoked salmon, Isle of Mull rainbow trout, and all kinds of fresh fish. I've named this seafood specialty for picturesque Oban.

4 tablespoons unsalted butter, cut up
2 tablespoons all-purpose flour
2 cups light cream or milk
1 teaspoon dried thyme
3 tablespoons chopped fresh dill or parsley
Salt, freshly ground pepper
3 large potatoes, cooked, peeled and sliced
1½ cups cooked green peas or cut-up green beans
1 pound white-fleshed fish (cod or flounder), fillets,
    cooked and cubed
2 tablespoons fresh lemon juice
½ cup fine dry bread crumbs

Preheat oven to 350 degrees. Butter bottom and sides of a shallow baking dish.

In a medium saucepan melt 2 tablespoons butter over medium-high heat. Stir in flour. Cook, stirring, 1 or 2 minutes. Gradually add cream or milk, stirring as adding, and cook, stirring until thickened and smooth, about 5 minutes. Add thyme and dill or parsley. Season with salt and pepper. Remove from heat.

Arrange half the potato slices in prepared dish. Top with half the peas or beans and half the fish cubes. Sprinkle with lemon juice. Repeat the layers. Pour prepared sauce over the vegetables and fish. Sprinkle with bread crumbs and remaining 2 tablespoons of butter, melted. Bake in preheated oven until bubbly hot and golden on top, about 30 minutes. 6 servings.

*Scene at harbor Oban, Scotland.*

# ❀ KEDGEREE

Kedgeree, a curry-laced creamy dish of rice, smoked or other fish, hard-cooked eggs, and seasonings, noted for its marvelous blend of flavors and textures, originated in India but was adopted and popularized by the English. Often served for breakfast in Scotland and Ireland, there are many versions of kedgeree. This one can be made with cod or salmon instead of the traditional finnan haddie (smoked haddock). Kedgeree is superb for entertaining as it's simple to prepare, can be made ahead, and reheated just before serving.

4 tablespoons unsalted butter, cut up
1 to 2 tablespoons curry powder
2 tablespoons fresh lemon juice
2½ cups cooked long-grain rice
2½ cups flaked cooked cod or salmon
2 teaspoons Worcestershire sauce
4 hard-cooked eggs, shelled and chopped
½ cup chopped fresh parsley
Salt, freshly ground pepper

In a large saucepan melt the butter over medium-high heat. Stir in the curry powder. Reduce the heat to medium-low; cook 1 minute. Add the lemon juice, rice, cod or salmon. Cook slowly, stirring, until the foods are heated, about 5 minutes. Add the chopped eggs and parsley. Season with salt and pepper. Leave on low heat long enough to heat all the ingredients. Serve shaped into a mound on a platter. 6 to 8 servings.

# ❀ BANTRY BAY MUSSEL STEW

In mid-May the town of Bantry, set on glorious Bantry Bay in Ireland's spectacular Southwest, celebrates its favorite seafood with an annual Mussel Fair. A favorite Irish way of cooking the salt-water mollusks is in a wine or cider-flavored sauce such as this one.

4 dozen mussels in shells
2 medium yellow onions, peeled and sliced thinly
1½ cups dry white wine or apple cider
1 teaspoon sugar
1 medium bay leaf
½ teaspoon dried thyme
2 tablespoons chopped fresh parsley
Salt, freshly ground pepper
¼ pound fresh mushrooms, cleaned and quartered
4 tablespoons unsalted butter, cut up
2 tablespoons fresh lemon juice
2 tablespoons all-purpose flour
Toast triangles from 4 slices firm white bread

Scrub mussels well and rinse under running water to remove all dirt. Remove beards just before cooking.

In a large pot combine the mussels, onions, wine or cider, sugar, bay leaf, thyme, and parsley. Season with salt and pepper. Cook, covered, over high heat until mussels open, about 8 minutes. Discard any unopened mussels. Remove from heat. Take out mussels; remove from shells. Strain mussel liquid; reserve.

In a small skillet sauté the mushrooms in 2 tablespoons butter and the lemon juice over medium heat for 4 minutes. Set aside.

In a large saucepan melt remaining 2 tablespoons butter. Stir in flour; cook, stirring, 1 to 2 minutes. Add strained mussel liquid and cook slowly, stirring, about 7 minutes, until sauce is smooth and thickened. Add cooked mussels and sautéed mushrooms and leave over heat long enough to heat through. Serve on toast triangles. 4 to 6 servings.

## ❀ DRESSED CRAB

Succulent crabs are plentiful in Scotland and Ireland and the tender meat is featured in many dishes. This is a version of deviled crab that is a good first course.

1 pound crabmeat, preferably lump, picked over
½ cup mayonnaise
1½ cups fresh bread crumbs
1 tablespoon fresh lemon juice
1 tablespoon Dijon-style mustard
1 teaspoon Worcestershire sauce
Salt, freshly ground pepper
3 tablespoons unsalted butter, cut up

In a medium bowl combine the crabmeat, mayonnaise, 1 cup bread crumbs, lemon juice, mustard, and Worcestershire. Season with salt and pepper. Mix to blend well. Spoon mixture into 6 crab shells or individual ramekins, dividing equally.

In a small skillet melt butter over medium-low heat. Add remaining ½ cup bread crumbs. Sauté 1 minute. Top each shell with some of the buttered crumbs. Refrigerate, covered, until ready to cook. Leave at room temperature 30 minutes before cooking.

To cook, preheat oven to 375 degrees. Place shells on a baking sheet. Bake in preheated oven until bubbly hot and golden brown, about 20 minutes. 6 servings.

# ❀ FISH AND CHIPS

"The Good Companions," as the late Sir Winston Churchill affectionately called fish and chips, have long been a popular Gaelic culinary duet, in fact an institution. The Scots and Irish dearly love to go to a Chip Shop or "Chippie" for "fish 'n' chips," sprinkled with salt and malt vinegar, and wrapped traditionally in a newspaper cornucopia.

So, what are fish and chips? Simply, they are strips of fish and potatoes fried in deep fat until golden and crisp. Sold as early as the mid-1800s as street snacks by vendors, generally women, they were offered together as easy and cheap hot meals for factory workers. But soon fish and chips were national favorites, eaten as street snacks or in pubs by everyone: socialites, young and old, singles and couples. And, it even became fashionable to serve these humble companions at aristocratic parties. While any firm, white-fleshed fish can be used, the favorite was haddock, as it remains today.

Fish and chips are simple to prepare and fun to serve and enjoy. This is my recipe for preparing them.

2 pounds all-purpose potatoes
2 pounds firm white-fleshed fish (haddock or cod)
1 cup all-purpose flour
Salt
1 large egg, beaten
⅓ cup milk
About ⅓ cup water
Shortening or vegetable oil for frying
Malt vinegar (optional)

Peel and slice potatoes. Cut into strips about 2½ inches long and 2 inches wide. Leave in cold water until ready to cook. Wash fish; wipe completely dry. Cut into strips or pieces about 3 × 3 inches.

Meanwhile, in a medium bowl combine flour, salt to taste, egg, milk, and water. Whisk until batter is smooth. Leave at room temperature about 30 to 40 minutes.

When ready to cook, heat shortening or oil in a deep-fat fryer to a temperature of 375 degrees. Wipe dry the potato strips and deep-fry them, several at a time, until golden and crisp. With a slotted spoon transfer to paper towels; let drain. Keep warm in a preheated 250-degree oven.

For the fish, whisk batter. Dip strips or pieces of fish in batter; let excess drain back into bowl. Fry, several at a time, in hot fat until just cooked through and golden and crisp, about 3 minutes per side. With a slotted spoon, transfer to paper towels; let drain. Keep warm while frying remaining fish.

To serve, arrange potatoes and fish on a platter. Pass salt and vinegar separately to be sprinkled over fish and chips. 4 servings.

# Poultry
# and
# Game

*Scottish Poulterer.*

101

> "A *Stoved Howtowdie wi' Drappit Eggs* and *Wee Grumphie* (suckling pig) *wi' Neeps* (turnips) were two dishes that delighted Penelope in *Penelope's Experiences in Scotland* (Kate Douglas Wiggan) in late Victorian times."
>
> — *The Scots Kitchen*

$P$ursuing the lore of Gaelic fare has led me over the years to the discovery of some bizarre and amusing names for old-time culinary specialties made with poultry and game. The repertoire of these traditional dishes, prepared and loved for generations, reaffirms the Scots' and Irish' keen senses of humor.

Who but the Gaels would have created fare called Bawd Bree (hare stew), Howtowdie Wi' Drappit Eggs (stuffed pot-roasted chicken with poached eggs), Roastit Bubbly-Jock (turkey stuffed with sausage and chestnuts), Wet Devil (chicken breasts in spicy mustard sauce), Coinin Tapaidh (fast rabbit), Spatchcock (chicken cooked in a hurry), Galloping Horseshoes (chicken-filled horseshoe-shaped pastries), or Dressy Lady (wine-flavored chicken casserole)?

It was in the heart of Scotland, a majestic area of mountains, lochs, rivers, and forests with bleak and beautiful moorlands known as the Trossachs, "bristly country," where I found and was reminded of the innovative Gaelic game dishes. For here superb wild game, such as the great red deer, and noble birds (especially the grouse, pheasant and partridge), are found in the Highlands' vast forests and moors.

This is also the land of Scotland's most colorful folk hero, Robert MacGregor, a robust and genial cateran whose 18th century epic adventures are depicted in the celebrated movie, *Rob Roy*, and were commemorated in Sir Walter Scott's novel, *Rob Roy*. He and his companions were known to have enjoyed a lot of bonny eating while on the run.

In *The Scots Kitchen* F. Marian McNeill has a recipe for a "romantically named dish," Rob Roy's Pleasure (Braised

Haunch of Venison), which the author enjoyed at a dinner in the Trossachs. McNeill wrote: "Whether cattle-raiding in the fertile "laigh countrie," or chasing the wild deer in the hills, it was unthinkable that the redoubtable Rob Roy should return with his followers lacking the wherewithal for a feast."

Enjoyed by generations of hunters and raiders, the succulent venison would be "Pot-roasted in a capacious three-legged pot, or braised with whatever vegetables and wild herbs lay to hand," McNeill declared.

While game was a great contribution to the diet in the past, and the Scots and Irish are still fond of dishes made with it, the Gaels have also been ardent devotees of a variety of poultry and game birds, which are still accorded places of honor on their dining tables. Both domesticated and wild species are deeply respected and sought-after fare in Scotland and Ireland.

Although Gaels have traditional favorite pies made with game or birds and elaborate holiday dishes featuring the duck and goose, a majority of recipes in this collection are for easily prepared specialties, with particular emphasis on poultry.

## ❀ DEVILED CHICKEN-BARLEY POT

Deviling, or flavoring with pungent seasonings such as spices and mustard or other condiments, was a common old technique of treating several foods, especially poultry. This one-dish specialty features deviled chicken breasts, barley, applesauce, and green peas. It's good for an informal pot-luck meal.

3 pounds boneless, skinless chicken breasts
½ cup (1 stick) unsalted butter, cut-up
1 cup finely chopped yellow onions
1 tablespoon fresh lemon juice
1 tablespoon Worcestershire sauce
2 tablespoons Dijon-style mustard
2 teaspoons curry powder
⅛ teaspoon cayenne pepper
Salt, freshly ground pepper
2 cups chicken broth
2 cups applesauce
6 cups cooked barley
4 cups frozen green peas
1 teaspoon dried garden mint
¼ cup chopped fresh parsley

With a sharp knife cut the chicken breasts into large cubes or bite-size pieces. Rinse; wipe dry.

In a large skillet melt the butter over medium-high heat. Add the onions. Sauté until translucent, about 5 minutes. Stir in the lemon juice, Worcestershire, mustard, curry powder, and cayenne pepper; mix well. Add the chicken pieces. Sauté for 5 minutes. Season with salt and pepper. Pour in chicken broth. Add the applesauce. Cook, covered, over medium-low heat for 10 minutes. Remove from heat. Spoon chicken mixture into a large casserole or ovenproof pot with a cover. (Can be prepared 1 day ahead. Cover and refrigerate.)

Preheat oven to 350 degrees.

Remove casserole or pot from the refrigerator. Leave at room temperature 30 minutes. Add barley, green peas, and mint. Mix well. Cook, covered, in preheated oven until bubbly hot, about 40 minutes. Serve garnished with the parsley. 12 servings.

# ❀ KILDARE CHICKEN IN A POT

Now known for its horses, race courses, and pastoral acres, County Kildare's first recorded inhabitants are a Celtic people who may have come to this area from Cornwall. They built great hill-forts, the remains of which can be seen at several sites, before the arrival of Christianity. Kildare Town is where the much-loved St. Bridget founded a 5th century religious settlement. The area is also noted for its thriving market towns and fine restaurants featuring poultry and game specialties. This is an adaptation of a farmhouse recipe.

1 whole chicken, about 3½ pounds
Salt, freshly ground pepper
¼ cup (½ stick) unsalted butter, cut up
2 tablespoons vegetable or olive oil
18 small white onions, peeled
3 large carrots, scraped and sliced thickly
½ cup chicken broth
1 teaspoon dried thyme
18 small new potatoes, peeled
1 pound whole fresh mushrooms, cleaned
½ cup chopped fresh parsley

Remove skin from chicken, if desired. Rinse; take out any excess fat; pat dry. Season inside with salt and pepper. Truss the chicken. In a large pot or casserole, heat the butter and oil over medium-high heat. Add the chicken; brown on all sides, turning over with two large spoons, until golden, about 10 minutes. Remove to a platter.

Add onions and carrots to drippings; sauté 5 minutes. Add chicken broth and thyme. Return chicken to pot. Cook, covered, over medium-low heat until tender, about 1 hour. Add potatoes after dish has been cooking 30 minutes; and mushrooms after 45 minutes. To serve, cut up chicken and place vegetables around it on a platter. Cover with sauce and sprinkle with parsley. 6 servings. (Partially cook the dish ahead and finish cooking just before serving).

## ✿ COTTAGE CHICKEN-HAM PIE

Irish cooks like to include ham or bacon in their farmhouse or cottage chicken dishes such as this tasty pie.

½ cup (1 stick) unsalted butter
½ cup finely chopped onions
¼ cup all-purpose flour
2 cups chicken broth
½ teaspoon dried thyme or marjoram
Salt, freshly ground pepper
2 cups cooked mixed vegetables (green peas or beans, broccoli)
1 cup diced cooked ham
3 cups cubed, cooked white meat of chicken
3 cups seasoned warm mashed potatoes
Paprika

Preheat oven to 425 degrees.
In a medium heavy saucepan melt the butter over medium-high heat. Add the onions; sauté until translucent, about 5 minutes. Stir in flour; cook 1 minute. Gradually add chicken broth, stirring as adding. Cook over medium low heat, stirring, until thickened and smooth, about 4 minutes. Add thyme or marjoram. Season with salt and pepper. Remove from heat.
In a 2½-quart casserole arrange vegetables, ham, and chicken in layers. Cover with the sauce. Top with mashed potatoes,

spreading evenly. Sprinkle with paprika, if desired. Bake in pre-heated oven until bubbly hot, about 25 minutes. 6 servings. (Cook beforehand and reheat in modern oven, if desired.)

## ❀ FRIAR'S CHICKEN

This old-time dish, served as a soup or one-dish meal, is said to have been created by cooks of the holy orders. H. V. Morton acclaimed it as a "great and romantic food," and "a dish to banish melancholy." After their famous "Journey To The Hebrides," Dr. Samuel Johnson and James Boswell included comments about the foods and dishes they encountered. It was on the Isle of Skye that they had for supper "a large dish of fricassee of fowl, I believe a dish called fried [or friar's] chicken or something like it. . . ," wrote Boswell. Here is my version of a modern fricassee.

1 frying chicken, about 2½ pounds, cut up
¼ cup (½ stick) unsalted butter
2 medium yellow onions, peeled and sliced
About 1 cup dry white wine or apple juice
½ teaspoon dried thyme
Salt, pepper to taste
¼ cup finely chopped ham
1 cup cut-up green peppers
3 tablespoons chopped fresh parsley

Rinse chicken pieces; dry. Set aside.
In a large skillet melt the butter over medium-high heat. Add onions. Sauté until translucent, about 5 minutes. Push aside. Add chicken pieces; cook on all sides until golden brown, about 8 minutes. Add wine or apple juice, and thyme. Season

with salt and pepper. Cook, covered, over medium-low heat for 25 minutes. Add the ham and green peppers. Continue cooking until chicken is tender, about 15 minutes. Stir in parsley. 4 servings. (Can be prepared partially 1 day ahead.)

## ❀ OVEN-FRIED OATED CHICKEN

This crisp, golden chicken, dipped in buttermilk and lemon juice, and coated with an herb seasoned oat-flour mixture before it's baked, is superb for indoor and outdoor meals. It can be eaten hot or cold.

12 chicken thighs
1 cup buttermilk
1 teaspoon Dijon-style mustard
1 tablespoon fresh lemon juice
Salt, freshly ground pepper
1 cup rolled oats
1 cup all-purpose flour
1 teaspoon curry powder
½ teaspoon paprika
About ⅓ cup melted butter

Remove skin from chicken thighs; rinse; pat dry. Place in a single layer in a large shallow dish.

Combine buttermilk, mustard, and lemon juice in a small dish. Season with salt and pepper. Mix well. Pour over chicken pieces. Turn them over to coat well. Refrigerate, covered with plastic wrap, 1 to 2 hours.

Combine the oats, flour, curry powder, and paprika, seasoned with salt and pepper, in a plastic bag. Shake to mix well.

Remove chicken thighs, one at a time, from marinade, draining off any excess marinade. Place, two or three at a time, into plastic bag with oat-flour mixture. Shake to coat well.

Meanwhile, preheat oven to 350 degrees. Brush a baking sheet with melted butter. Place chicken pieces, allowing a little space between each one, on buttered sheet. Bake in preheated oven, turning once, until cooked and golden, about 1 hour. 12 servings.

## ❀ HIBERNIAN CIDER-FLAVORED CHICKEN

Hibernia is the Latin name for Ireland. This braised chicken dish, flavored with cider and mushrooms, is made with typical Irish foods.

1 frying chicken, about 3 pounds, cut up
Salt, freshly ground pepper
All-purpose flour
3 to 4 tablespoons unsalted butter
1 thin slice bacon, diced
1 medium leek, white part only, cleaned and sliced
1 cup sliced fresh mushrooms
1 cup heavy cream
½ cup apple cider
Fresh watercress leaves

Rinse chicken pieces; wipe dry. Pull off and discard skin. Season with salt and pepper. Dip each chicken piece in flour to coat lightly on all sides.

In a large skillet melt the butter over medium-high heat. Add chicken pieces and brown on all sides. With tongs, remove to a plate and keep warm.

Add the bacon and leeks to drippings. Sauté until tender, about 5 minutes. Add mushrooms; sauté 3 minutes. Return chicken pieces to the skillet. Pour in cream and cider. Reduce heat to medium-low. Cook, covered, until chicken is tender, about 35 minutes. Season with salt and pepper, if desired. Serve garnished with watercress leaves. 4 servings. (This dish can be partially made ahead and cooked just before serving.)

## ❁ STOVED CHICKEN

This traditional Scottish Highland specialty is also called *Stovies*. The word comes from the French *etuver*, meaning to cook in an enclosed pot. The typical slow cooking method thus preserves the flavors of the ingredients.

1 broiler-fryer chicken, about 3 pounds, cut up
About ½ cup unsalted butter
2 large onions, halved lengthwise, sliced thin
4 medium potatoes, peeled and sliced thickly
Salt, freshly ground pepper
1½ cups hot chicken broth
¼ cup chopped fresh parsley

Preheat oven to 350 degrees.
Rinse chicken pieces; wipe dry. In a large heavy skillet melt ¼ cup butter over medium-high heat. Add chicken pieces, a few at a time. Sauté, turning once, until golden brown on all sides. With tongs remove to a platter. Melt remaining ¼ cup butter in skillet. Add onion and potato slices; sauté 5 minutes. Spoon half the sautéed vegetables with butter drippings into a large pot or casserole. Season with salt and pepper. Top with sautéed chicken pieces and remaining vegetables. Season with salt and

pepper. Pour in hot broth. Cook slowly, covered, in preheated oven until chicken is tender, about 1 hour. Serve chicken pieces and vegetables, sprinkled with parsley and with sauce spooned over them. 4 to 6 servings.

## ❀ GOLDEN CHICKEN CROQUETTES

During the Auld Alliance Scots became devotees of many French-inspired dishes including the croquette, a name derived from *croquet*, to crunch. These creamy morsels in their golden shell of crisp, deep-fried crumbs make excellent party fare, since they can be made up ahead of time and cooked just before serving.

3 cups diced, cooked white meat of chicken
1 medium onion, peeled and minced
½ cup minced celery
½ cup minced green pepper
½ teaspoon dried sage
Salt, freshly ground pepper
3 tablespoons unsalted butter
3 tablespoons all-purpose flour
1 cup chicken broth
¼ cup light cream
⅛ teaspoon cayenne pepper
Fine dry bread crumbs
2 eggs, beaten
Fat or vegetable oil for frying

In a meat grinder or food processor, with metal blade in place, grind or purée the chopped chicken, onion, celery, green pepper, and sage. Season with salt and pepper. Turn into a large bowl.

In a medium heavy saucepan melt the butter over medium-high heat. Stir in flour. Cook, stirring, 2 minutes. Gradually pour in chicken broth. Cook slowly, stirring often, until sauce is thickened and smooth, about 6 minutes. Add the cream and cayenne. Season with salt and pepper. Remove from the heat. Add to chicken mixture; mix well.

Spread evenly in a flat dish and chill in refrigerator 1½ to 2 hours. With the hands, shape into ovals or rectangles. Roll in bread crumbs to cover lightly. Dip in beaten egg. Roll again in bread crumbs and pat with a knife. Place on a plate or a baking pan. Chill in refrigerator for a few hours or overnight. Before cooking, allow to stand at room temperature for 1 hour.

Fry in deep hot fat (375 degrees), turning once or twice, until golden brown. Drain on paper towels. Serve at once. An attractive way to serve the croquettes is to pile them on a napkin in a pyramid or mound, garnished with watercress or strips of raw vegetables. 6 to 8 servings.

# ❋ "SMOTHERED" TURKEY WITH WALNUTS

A native of Persia, the large wrinkled walnut, a name derived from "wealh," meaning strange or foreign, became erroneously known as "English walnut" because the nuts were carried around the world in English trading ships. In Gaelic lands walnuts came to be associated with feast day dishes as they were thought to bring good luck and good health.

Specialties called "smothered" included foods mixed or covered with other foods, a kind of hash. This one can be made easily from leftover turkey. Serve with a green salad and warm scones or soda bread for a brunch or supper.

2 tablespoons unsalted butter
½ cup finely chopped onion
½ cup finely chopped celery
1 teaspoon curry powder
½ teaspoon paprika
1 cup stale coarse bread crumbs
4 cups diced cooked turkey
½ cup turkey gravy
Salt, freshly ground pepper
1 cup coarsely chopped walnuts
½ cup heavy or light cream
½ cup chopped fresh parsley

In a large heavy skillet melt butter over medium-high heat. Add onion and celery. Sauté until vegetables are soft, about 5 minutes. Stir in curry powder and paprika; sauté 1 minute. Add bread crumbs; sauté until golden brown, about 5 minutes.

Add turkey and gravy to mixture in skillet. Season with salt and pepper. Reduce heat to medium-low. Cook, covered, to blend flavors, about 10 minutes. Stir walnuts, cream, and parsley into turkey mixture. Increase heat to medium-high. Cook, stirring occasionally, until heated through, about 5 minutes. To serve, spoon into a serving dish. 4 to 6 servings. (This dish can be partially made ahead and cooked just before serving.)

## ❀ SUMMER LUNCHEON CHICKEN SALAD

Serve this easy-to-prepare salad for a luncheon entrée or a buffet specialty.

3 cups diced, cooked white meat of chicken
½ cup mayonnaise
½ cup sour cream
2 to 3 teaspoons curry powder
½ cup coarsely chopped walnuts
Salt, freshly ground pepper
About 6 green lettuce leaves, washed and dried
2 hard-cooked eggs, shelled and cut into wedges
2 large ripe tomatoes, peeled and cut into wedges
2 dill pickles, sliced lengthwise

In a large bowl combine the diced chicken, mayonnaise, sour cream, curry powder, and walnuts. Season with salt and pepper. Toss with two spoons to mix well. Refrigerate, covered with plastic wrap, 1 hour or up to 6 hours, to blend flavors. When ready to serve, arrange lettuce leaves on a platter. Spoon salad over them. Garnish with egg and tomato wedges and pickle slices. 6 servings.

# ❀ BRAISED DUCKLING WITH TURNIPS

Originally from Brittany, a rugged peninsula in northwestern France noted for its Celtic cuisine and culture, this recipe features duck braised with lightly caramelized turnips, which absorb some of the fat and sauce, giving the vegetables an inviting, different flavor. In America it can be prepared with a Long Island duckling, sold ready to cook and usually frozen. Serve for a special company dinner.

4 to 5-pound duckling, thawed
Salt
¾ cup apple juice or dry white wine
2 cups beef broth
1 bouquet garni (2 sprigs parsley, ¼ teaspoon dried thyme,
    1 bay leaf, tied in cheesecloth)
Freshly ground pepper
3 tablespoons unsalted butter
3 turnips (about 1 pound), peeled and cubed
16 small white onions, peeled
1 tablespoon sugar

Preheat oven to 450 degrees.
Rinse duckling; drain and pat dry. Rub with salt inside and out. Prick skin all over with a fork. Place on a rack in a roasting pan. Cook 20 minutes in preheated oven. Reduce heat to 350 degrees. Remove duckling from oven to a platter. Pour off fat, reserving 2 tablespoons for sauce. Add apple juice or wine, broth, bouquet garni, and pepper to the fat in the pan, mixing well. Return duckling to pan; place in oven. Cook until desired degree of doneness and skin is crisp and brown, about 1½ hours.

Meanwhile, in a medium heavy skillet melt butter over medium-high heat. Add turnips and onions. Sauté for 5 minutes. Add sugar and cook another 2 minutes, turning to coat vegetables. Arrange vegetables around duckling 30 minutes before the roasting time is completed. Baste duck and vegetables with the sauce. When cooked, transfer duckling to a platter and carve. Serve surrounded with the vegetables. Spoon any drippings or sauce over them. 4 servings.

## ❀ MICHAELMAS GOOSE

In Ireland, the autumn celebration of Michaelmas Day, September 29th, has long been observed with the eating of a roast goose, traditionally stuffed with potatoes. There is an old Irish saying that if you eat goose on St. Michael's Day you will never want for money all year round. Since autumn is also the time of year for picking apples, goose was served with applesauce, and often followed by baked apples or an apple tart for dessert. In this recipe apples are included in the stuffing.

STUFFING:
2 cups chopped onions
3 cups chopped peeled tart apples
2 cups stale bread cubes
1 cup coarsely chopped walnuts (optional)
¼ cup apple juice or cider
Salt, freshly ground pepper

In a large bowl combine the onions, apples, bread cubes, walnuts, and apple juice or cider. Season with salt and pepper.

1 goose (10 to 12 pounds)
Juice of 1 lemon
Salt, freshly ground pepper

Preheat oven to 325 degrees.

Rinse the goose; pat dry. Prick skin all over with a fork. Rub with lemon juice inside and out. Sprinkle with salt and pepper inside and out. Fill cavities with the stuffing; close with skewers. Truss. Place goose, breast side up, on a rack in a large roasting pan. Roast in preheated oven until tender, about 3½ hours, allowing 15 to 20 minutes per pound. During the cooking, remove occasionally any accumulated fat in the pan and turn goose from side to side once or twice. When cooked, transfer goose to a platter. Let stand 30 minutes before carving. Serve with stuffing alongside the goose. 6 to 8 servings.

## ❀ SCOTCH RED GROUSE

For many gastronomes, the greatest treasure of all birds is the grouse. Although there are several species—the capercailzie or wood, ptarmigan or white, and the black—the most highly prized is the red, called simply grouse or Scotch grouse, which is found on the moorlands of Scotland. The first grouse that falls each year on August 12 heralds the opening of the shooting season, and ardent guns from all over the world come to bag them, a sport reserved for privileged, well-heeled participants. The grouse have a particular gamey individual flavor achieved from dining on heather and are most often cooked stuffed with a handful of whortleberries or cranberries. As is also the case with pheasant, they are made into superb pies.

4 young grouse, dressed
4 thin slices bacon
⅓ to ½ cup unsalted butter
1½ cups meat or chicken broth
Salt, freshly ground pepper
2 tablespoons all-purpose flour
1½ cups light cream
3 to 4 tablespoons red currant or raspberry jelly

Rinse birds; drain and pat dry. Wrap a slice of bacon around each bird and secure with a skewer. In a large skillet melt butter over medium-high heat. Add birds and fry, turning once, until golden on all sides. Pour in broth. Season with salt and pepper. Reduce heat to medium-low. Cook slowly, covered, until tender, about 30 minutes, the exact time depending on the age of the birds. Remove birds to a platter and keep warm. Scrape up the drippings. Add flour; mix well. Pour in cream and cook over medium-high heat, stirring, until thickened and smooth. Stir in jelly. Correct the seasoning. When cooked, transfer birds to a platter. Cut into halves. Pour a little sauce over them. Serve remainder of sauce in a bowl. 4 servings.

# Meats

*Near Killagin, Kerry. A young boy with donkey,*
*dog and peat baskets.*

*"The Celts sit on dried grass and have their meals served on wooden tables raised slightly above the earth. Their food consists of a small number of loaves of bread together with a large amount of meat, either boiled or roasted on charcoal or on spits. They partake of this in a cleanly but leonine fashion, raising up whole limbs in both hands and cutting off the meat, while any part which is hard to tear off they cut through with a small dagger . . .*

*When a large number dine together they sit around in a circle with the most influential men in the centre. . . ,"* says Cicero's tutor Posidonius, who visited Britain about 110 B.C.

One has only to stir the imagination to envisage the protocol at these lengthy feasts. For even the joints of meat were served in a bizarre hierarchical order. While the best portion was given to a champion warrior, the king rated a thigh; the queen, a haunch; a young lord, a leg; and heads went to charioteers.

Meat, along with milk and cheese, formed the main part of the Celtic diet. While pork was the favorite kind, the preference for feasts, mutton or lamb and venison also were commonly eaten. Cattle, however, were kept primarily for milk.

Like the Celts, the Gaels have been ingenious in using not only the flesh but all parts of animals, together with other compatible ingredients, in the creation of distinctive national dishes. Meat in one form or another is the primary component of a Gaelic meal.

A major early influence on the cookery was the introduction of an iron cauldron in which different meats could be combined with any available foods to be cooked slowly. Until electrification brought stoves to rural kitchens, in almost all homes the principal cooking utensil was an all-purpose cast-iron pot, which had been used in varying form since the time of the Celts. Just about everything that most families ate was cooked in this three-legged pot over a wood or peat fire out in the open or in the hearth. Thus began the Gaelic tradition of enjoying nourishing one-pot meals.

The Celts also understood the important art of preserving meats by salting and brining, enabling them to eat during the long cold winters such staples known now as sausages, bacon or rashers, hams, black and white puddings, and corned brisket, among others.

The Gaelic practice of making small amounts of food go a long way and for utilizing leftovers has resulted in any number of innovative savory puddings, pies, loaves, and pasties.

'Tis true that the Scots favor meat innards, especially in their notorious national dish, a sausage called haggis, and that the Irish relish a flavorful pig's head brawn. Gaels have excelled in the art of preparing what one may call miscellaneous meats. The number and variety of dishes created with the diverse parts defy one's imagination. A treasured Scotch soup called *Powsowdie* is made with a sheep's head. Shin of beef was the main ingredient of *pottit hough* and the meat of sheep's trotters goes into a collection of concoctions, from fritters to soups. Whereas a complex Irish specialty, Collared Head, traditionally eaten on St. Stephen's Day, December 26, is made from a salted pig's head, vegetables, and seasonings.

One of the best places to experience the richness of the Gaelic meat larder is Cork City, which, with its deep harbor and fertile adjacent farmlands, was well known in earlier times for its variety of foods, especially the butter produced there. Here in its lively 18th century covered market are curiosities proving that in Cork the people have found everything but the "oink" of the pig edible.

A tour, however, is a bit puzzling with lots of surprises. Drisheen, a long grayish-purple sausage is actually an herb-flavored black or blood pudding, which, when sliced, is fried or grilled and eaten for breakfast. Other oddities named "skirts" and "bodices" were none other than fluted pig trimmings and pickled spareribs, prominently displayed next to pigs' tails. But, on a recent visit what really caught my eye were the trotters or pigs' feet that the Irish call *cruibíns* or *crubeens*, pronounced "crew beans." "They're buying the hind ones; they have more meat. The front ones are bony," my guide explained.

But in a pub, what kind we ate didn't seem to matter. Once a staple family food, the trotters are still sold pickled at country horse races and in some informal eateries where they are savored when picked up with the fingers, nibbled, and washed down with the last pint.

Included here is a selection from the Gaelic meat repertoire that reflects the interesting diversity of the native dishes.

## ❀ BEEF TARTARE

A popular pub specialty made with raw ground beef and piquant seasonings is called beefsteak or beef tartare, a name believed to have derived from the nomadic Tartar practice of scraping and eating raw meats. Celts also enjoyed a similar preparation, made with such flavorings as garlic and onions. Served now as a starter or snack, many Gaels believe that the meat mixture is also a fine restorative after a night of celebrating.

2 pounds freshly ground lean beef sirloin*
4 raw egg yolks*
½ cup minced onions
¼ cup chopped fresh parsley
4 teaspoons capers, drained
2 tablespoons Worcestershire sauce
2 tablespoons Dijon-style mustard
Salt, freshly ground pepper
8 slices dark brown bread, toasted

GARNISHES:
1 medium red onion, sliced and separated into rings
2 tomatoes, peeled, cut into wedges
16 cucumber and pickle slices

Place the beef in a large bowl. Add, one at a time, the egg yolks, onions, parsley, capers, Worcestershire sauce, and mustard. Season with salt and pepper. Mix to thoroughly combine the ingredients. Shape into a large loaf or two patties. Refrigerate, covered with plastic wrap, until ready to serve. (Prepare 1 hour before serving). To serve, place on a wooden board, tray or platter, surrounded by slices of toast and separate dishes of any desired number of the garnishes. 8 servings.
*Be very careful about the ground beef and eggs you buy for this dish. To purchase the foods, choose a reliable butcher and ask that the beef be ground twice shortly before buying and serving it. The eggs and meat should be as fresh as possible.

## ❀ CORNED BEEF 'N' CABBAGE

Ah, to be sure! This hearty dinner-in-a-pot has become a celebrated specialty for Irish-Americans on St. Patrick's Day. But originally the dish was a traditional Easter Sunday dinner in Ireland. For the beef, which was salted or brined during the winter to preserve it, was eaten after the long, meatless Lenten fast. Later, it was a traditional Sunday lunch for Dubliners. Serve for an Irish holiday or special-occasion meal.

1 lean corned beef brisket (about 4 pounds), trimmed of
   excess fat
1 peeled medium yellow onion, stuck with 4 whole cloves
1 teaspoon dry mustard
½ teaspoon dried thyme
Freshly ground pepper
3 medium yellow onions, peeled and cut in halves
4 large carrots, scraped and sliced thickly
6 medium all-purpose potatoes, peeled and halved
1 medium (about 2 pounds), green cabbage, outer leaves
   removed, cored and cut into wedges

Place the beef in a large pot. Add enough water to cover the meat by 2 inches. Bring to a boil on high heat. Lower heat to medium-low. Skim and discard any froth that rises to the top. Add onion stuck with cloves, mustard, thyme, and pepper.

Cook slowly, covered, according to package instructions or until meat is tender and can be easily pierced with a fork, about 3 hours. Add onions, carrots, potatoes, and cabbage during the last 30 minutes of cooking. Remove and discard onion stuck with cloves. Take out beef. Cover with aluminum foil; keep warm. Allow meat to rest 20 to 30 minutes before carving. To serve, cut into slices and place in center of a platter. Arrange vegetables around it. Top with some of the broth, if desired. 6 to 8 servings.

# ✻ PAT'S CORNED BEEF HASH

I gathered with a few fellow writers late one Sunday morning at Pat's abode for a couple of eye-openers, lively conversation, and a plate of his hearty browned, crusty *haché*. We wondered about our Irish pal who used a French name for his appetizing fare. Later, I learned that the cooking term "hash" does indeed come from the French *hachér*, meaning to chop, and the dish has a gastronomic pedigree. So, here's to Pat and his *haché*, a great winter treat.

1 large yellow onion, peeled and chopped
4 cups cooked or 2 cans (12 ounces each) corned beef, chopped
4 cups diced, peeled, boiled potatoes
½ teaspoon dried thyme or oregano
¼ cup chopped fresh parsley
Salt, freshly ground pepper
3 to 4 tablespoons unsalted butter
½ cup light cream or milk
8 warm poached eggs, drained (optional)
Warm chili sauce or ketchup

In a large bowl combine the chopped onion, corned beef, potatoes, thyme or oregano, and parsley. Season with salt and pepper. Mix well. When ready to cook, melt 3 tablespoons butter in a large skillet. Add beef mixture; press down firmly with a spatula. Cook over medium-high heat until a crust forms on the bottom. Turn with a spatula so that some of the crust is brought to the top. Add cream or milk, and continue cooking, turning the mixture, until browned and crisp, about 12 minutes. Serve in portions, each topped with a poached egg and a little chili sauce or ketchup, if desired. 8 servings. (The hash can be made partially beforehand and reheated).

# ❋ FARMHOUSE LAMB PIE

The Gaels have long been devotees of great meat pies that are prepared in various forms and then baked. In Scotland and Ireland you can find the dish year-round on dining tables, in pubs, and at outdoor events. One of the most traditional and commonly served is Shepherd's Pie, made originally with left-over roast lamb, gravy, and onion, and topped with mashed potatoes. Now subject to many variations and sometimes called cottage pie, this is yet another one that I enjoyed in a bed and breakfast, once a Highland farmhouse.

3 slices thin bacon, chopped
1 medium yellow onion, peeled and sliced
2 cups brown gravy
1 tablespoon Worcestershire sauce
½ teaspoon dried marjoram
Salt, freshly ground pepper
3 cups diced cooked lamb
2 cups seasoned mashed potatoes
2 tablespoons unsalted butter
½ teaspoon paprika

Preheat oven to 425 degrees.

In a medium skillet fry bacon over medium-high heat until crisp. Remove; drain on paper towels; set aside. Take out all but 1 tablespoon of left-over drippings from the skillet. Add the onion. Sauté until translucent, about 5 minutes. Stir in the gravy, Worcestershire sauce, and marjoram. Season with salt and pepper. Cook slowly 2 minutes to blend flavors.

Spoon the lamb into a 2½-quart casserole. Top with the onion-gravy mixture and bacon. Spoon the mashed potatoes, spreading evenly, over the ingredients. Dot with butter. Sprinkle with paprika. Bake in preheated oven until bubbly hot, about 25 minutes. 6 servings. (The pie can be made partially ahead and reheated.)

## ❀ DUBLIN CODDLE

Ireland's capital and largest city has two names, Dublin and *Baile Artha Cliath,* meaning City of the Hurdles, which was bestowed by Celtic traders in the $2^{nd}$ century A.D. The first early Celtic habitation was on the banks of the River Liffey. Now the National Museum in Dublin has the largest collection of Celtic antiquities in the world.

One of the oldest Dublin dishes, enjoyed by Sean O'Casey and James Joyce, is this simple stew which combines sausages and bacon, two of Ireland's favorite meats, and potatoes. Once a traditional Saturday night supper, eaten when the men came home from the pub, the nourishing, warming, and economical dish was washed down with mugs of stout. Coddle means slow cooking and some modern recipes include other foods such as apples and cider.

1½ pounds pork sausages, cut into chunks
1½ pounds smoked ham or bacon, cut into pieces
1 quart boiling water
2 large yellow onions, peeled and sliced thinly
2 pounds all-purpose potatoes (6 medium), peeled and
    sliced thickly
Salt, pepper to taste
3 tablespoons chopped fresh parsley

Preheat oven to 350 degrees.

Place cut-up sausages, ham or bacon pieces, and water in a large pot. Boil, covered, 5 minutes. Drain, reserving the liquid. Spoon meats into a casserole or ovenproof dish. Add onions and potatoes. Season with salt and pepper. Add enough of the reserved broth to cover the ingredients. Cook, covered, in preheated oven for 1 hour, removing the cover during the last 30 minutes. Ingredients should be cooked but not be mushy. Serve hot with vegetables over the meats. Soda bread is a traditional accompaniment. 8 servings. Make ahead and reheat, if desired.

## ❀ SCOTTISH MINCE COLLOPS

*"As soon as the collops were ready . . . Cluny gave them, with his own hand, a squeeze of lemon . . . They are such as I gave his Royal Highness [Prince Charles Edward Stuart] in this very house."*

— **Robert Louis Stevenson, *Kidnapped* 1886**

Collops, also collops-in-the-pan, or escalopes are thin slices of meat or game that Scots cook in a piquant sauce. Given the status of a national dish by Meg Dods, the eccentric innkeeper character in Sir Walter Scott's novel of Scottish social life, *St. Ronan's Wall*, recipes for collops appear in several old cookbooks. Minced collops, made with minced or ground meat, was a favorite Highland supper dish.

3 tablespoons rolled oats
2 tablespoons unsalted butter
1 large yellow onion, peeled and chopped
1½ pounds lean ground beef or lamb
½ cup beef broth
1 tablespoon cider vinegar
2 to 3 teaspoons curry powder
Salt, freshly ground pepper

Spread oats in an ungreased small skillet. Cook over medium-high heat about 3 minutes, stirring occasionally, until edges are light golden brown. Remove from heat; cool.

In a large skillet melt butter over medium-high heat. Add onion. Sauté until translucent, about 5 minutes. Add beef or lamb. Cook, stirring often, until redness disappears, about 10 minutes. Add broth, toasted oats, vinegar, and curry powder. Season with salt and pepper. Cook, covered, until meat is cooked, about 12 minutes. Serve with mashed potatoes, if desired, for a family supper. 6 servings. (Cook ahead and reheat, if desired.)

## ❀ BLARNEY CHEESE BURGERS

*The Gift of the Blarney:*
*"'Tis only found in Ireland*
*Where leprechauns all roam*
*And those who seek the crock of Gold*
*First kiss the Blarney Stone."*

The small village of Blarney, northwest of Cork City, is world famous because of its Blarney Stone, reputed to possess a unique power of bestowing the fabled "gift of gab." But to get it one must hike up a hill to the Blarney Castle ruin, climb 127 curved stone steps to the parapet, lie down, lean your head way back, and upside down, kiss the magical stone. Lo, you have been blessed by its ancient fairy spell.

Blarney is also the name of a Kerrygold aromatic cheese which has been slow-smoked over natural oak fires. Excellent to eat as is or use for cooking, the cheese has an appealing semi-soft texture.

1½ pounds lean ground beef or lamb
3 tablespoons vegetable oil
1 medium yellow onion, peeled and chopped
2 cups shredded green cabbage
⅓ cup shredded carrot
1 teaspoon dried mint (optional)
Salt, freshly ground pepper
6 hamburger rolls, split and toasted
⅓ cup Dijon-style or honey mustard
6 slices Kerrygold Irish Blarney or Swiss cheese

Shape the beef or lamb, preferably freshly ground, into 6 patties. In a large heavy skillet heat 1½ tablespoons oil over medium-high heat. Add the patties. Fry, turning once, until well browned, about 6 minutes. Drain on paper towels. Keep warm.

Heat remaining 1½ tablespoons oil in the skillet over medium heat. Add onion; sauté 1 minute. Add cabbage, carrot, and mint. Season with salt and pepper. Cook, covered, stirring occasionally, just until the vegetables are wilted, about 4 minutes.

When ready to cook, preheat broiler. Spread each bottom roll half with mustard. Place a patty on top. Cover with cabbage mixture, dividing evenly, and top with a slice of cheese. Place under broiler and broil until cheese is melted and bubbly hot, about 2 minutes. Cover with top roll and serve at once. 6 servings.

# ❀ GAELIC STEAKS

For a special small dinner, prepare these steaks with Scotch whisky if you're a Scot, or Irish whiskey if you're Irish. If neither, take your choice.

¼ cup (½ stick) unsalted butter
1 large yellow onion, peeled, cut crosswise and sliced thinly
4 center-cut fillet steaks
Freshly ground pepper to taste
½ cup beef broth
4 shots Scotch whisky or Irish whiskey
Sprigs of watercress

In a large skillet melt the butter over medium-high heat. Add onion slices. Sauté until translucent, about 5 minutes. With a slotted spoon remove to a plate and keep warm. Add steaks to drippings and sear over high heat 1 minute on each side. Reduce heat to medium and cook steaks about 4 minutes on each side for medium-rare. Remove to warm plates. Increase heat to high. Add beef broth, stirring and scraping up all browned bits on the bottom. Cook 2 to 3 minutes, until sauce is reduced by half. Season with pepper. Add whisky or whiskey. Heat 1 minute. Pour over steaks. Serve garnished with sautéed onions and watercress. 4 servings. (Prepare partially ahead, if desired.)

# ❀ BEEF STEW WITH STOUT

Laced with stout to give it a marvelous flavoring, this is a good do-ahead dish. It's easy to prepare and superb when reheated. While some versions are baked in the oven, this one is cooked on top of the stove.

2 pounds lean boneless beef, cut into ¾-to-1-inch cubes
Salt, freshly ground pepper
3 tablespoons vegetable oil
2 large yellow onions, peeled, cut in halves, sliced thinly
3 large carrots, scraped, sliced thickly
2 cloves garlic, peeled and chopped (optional)
3 tablespoons all-purpose flour
½ cup beef broth
1 bottle (12 ounces) stout (such as Guinness) or dark ale
2 medium bay leaves
½ teaspoon dried thyme
¼ cup chopped fresh parsley

Cut any fat from beef cubes. Sprinkle with salt and pepper. In a large heavy skillet heat oil over medium-high heat. Add beef cubes; brown on all sides, about 8 minutes. With a slotted spoon, transfer to a large bowl. Reduce heat to medium-low. Add sliced onions, carrots, and garlic to skillet; mix to coat vegetables with pan drippings. Stir in flour. Pour in broth and stout or ale. Add beef cubes with any juices, bay leaves, and thyme. Reduce heat to low and gently simmer, covered, stirring occasionally, until beef is tender and sauce is thickened, about 1½ hours. Remove and discard bay leaves. Season with salt and pepper, if desired. Serve, garnished with parsley. Or, cool, refrigerate, and reheat before serving. Boiled potatoes are a traditional accompaniment. 6 servings.

# ❀ HERBED OAT MEAT LOAF

The Gaels have long been exceedingly fond of loaves made with "mince" (a colloquialism for ground, or "minced" meat) that are traditionally served either hot or cold not only for home meals but for picnics and in pubs. This nourishing meat loaf is a good entrée for a family or company supper.

2 pounds meat loaf mixture (beef, veal and pork) or ground beef
1 cup toasted rolled oats*
½ cup milk
½ cup minced onions
½ cup minced celery
2 large eggs, beaten
½ cup chopped fresh parsley
1 teaspoon dried herbs (savory, basil, oregano or marjoram)
Salt, freshly ground pepper
3 slices thin bacon

*See page 24, Ayrshire Sausage Squares.

Preheat oven to 350 degrees. Grease a 9 × 5 × 3-inch loaf pan.

In a large bowl combine meat loaf mixture or beef, oats, milk, onions, celery, beaten eggs, parsley, and herbs. Season with salt and pepper. Mix thoroughly. Pack into prepared pan. Top with bacon slices, arranging lengthwise over loaf. Bake in preheated oven until loaf shrinks from edges of pan, about 1 hour. Spoon off any drippings. With two broad spatulas, transfer to a serving dish. To serve, cut into thick slices. Serve hot or cold. 6 servings.

# ❋ DONEGAL IRISH STEW

Donegal (pronounced downy-gaul), Ireland's northernmost county facing the Atlantic, is a ruggedly beautiful and mystic land, tucked away from the modern world. In the West is the Gaeltacht region where Irish (Gaelic) is still spoken and ancient traditions fiercely protected. It's also famous sheep country and the mutton and lamb produced here are the basis for many fine dishes, including this stew. Now prepared in many versions, the classic one is made simply by layering lamb, potatoes, and onions, flavored with thyme and parsley, into a casserole, covering the ingredients with cold water, and simmering until all is tender.

3 pounds breast of lamb
6 medium (about 2 pounds) all-purpose potatoes, peeled
    and sliced
5 medium yellow onions, peeled and sliced
½ teaspoon dried thyme
Salt, freshly ground pepper
2 to 3 cups cold water
3 tablespoons chopped fresh parsley

Preheat oven to 350 degrees.
Remove any fat from the lamb and cut into large cubes. In a heavy 4 to 5 quart casserole, arrange a layer of potatoes, and top with a layer of onions and then lamb. Season each layer with thyme, salt and pepper. Repeat the layers, topping with a thick layer of potatoes. Press down to compact layers. Pour in enough water to cover the ingredients. Cover and cook in preheated oven until ingredients are cooked, 2¼ to 2½ hours. Add a little more water during the cooking, if needed. The bottom layers of potatoes and onions will dissolve, absorbing meat juices to make a

thick sauce. Before serving, sprinkle with parsley. 4 to 6 servings. (The dish can be made ahead and reheated just before serving.)

## ✿ BRIDIES

Almost every weekend throughout the year there are Highland Games and Gatherings of the Scottish Clans taking place somewhere in the United States and Canada. Although the origins of the first games are lost in history, it's believed that they began in Scotland in the 11th century. The most famous now is the Highland Gathering held in Braemar, a Scottish Tayside resort town, in September. Along with all the pageantry and sports, there's also bonny eating of traditional fare. A favorite specialty is the beloved pastry turnover with a beef filling that is commonly called a bridie. It came originally from Forfar in Angus and the tasty pie is believed to have been created by a baker called Mr. Jolly.

Here's my recipe for it. Bridies are great for games or picnics.

FILLING:
1 pound lean round or flank steak, fat removed
⅔ cup minced beef suet*
1 medium yellow onion, peeled and minced
Salt, freshly ground pepper

Pound meat with a pounder to tenderize. Cut into thin strips and then ¼-inch cubes. In a medium bowl combine the minced suet and onion. Season with salt and pepper. Makes about 4 cups.

*Suet, the hard fat around beef kidneys, is available at super-markets. Ask a butcher to sell you a small amount.

PASTRY:
3 cups all-purpose flour
¾ teaspoon salt
½ cup lard or vegetable shortening
½ cup (1 stick) unsalted butter, cut up
About 5 tablespoons cold water
1 egg, beaten (for topping)
Salt, freshly ground pepper

Preheat oven to 400 degrees.

In a large bowl combine the flour and salt. With a pastry blender cut in lard or shortening and butter until mixture is like fine crumbs. Add cold water, enough to make a stiff dough. Gather into a ball. Turn out on a lightly floured surface. Divide the dough into 4 equal-size pieces. Roll each piece of dough into an 8-inch round.

Place about 1 cup or ¼ of the beef filling on half the circle, leaving a border. Gently fold the other half over, being careful not to tear the dough. Dampen edge of dough with cold water; press edges firmly together, crimping between your thumb and index finger or with a fork. Repeat for remaining 3 rounds.

Make 2 small holes in top of each turnover to allow steam to escape while baking. Place on an ungreased baking sheet. Brush tops with beaten egg.

Bake in a preheated oven for 20 minutes; reduce heat to 350 degrees and continue to bake until pastry is golden brown and flaky, about 30 minutes longer. Remove to a wire rack. Allow to cool slightly, about 5 minutes. Serve warm. Or allow to cool and serve cold. To reheat, put in a 350-degree oven for 10 minutes. Makes 4.

# ❀ LIMERICK BRAISED HAM

Once Limerick City on the Shannon River was world-famous for its lean and flavorful ham with a characteristic flavor acquired from being smoked over juniper branches. Now Limerick is better known as the setting for Frank McCourt's 1996 memoir, *Angela's Ashes*, and, of course, the nonsensical verse of five anapestic lines called a limerick. Also, the city's Hunt Museum has the finest collection of Celtic treasures outside the above mentioned National Museum in Dublin.

Prepare this baked specialty with Limerick or any other good kind of ham.

2 center-cut fully cooked ham slices, 1-inch thick
  (about 3 pounds)
2 tablespoons unsalted butter
1 medium yellow onion, peeled and minced
½ cup apple cider or juice
2 medium tart apples, peeled, cored and diced
3 tablespoons brown sugar
1 teaspoon Dijon-style mustard
⅛ teaspoon ground cloves
Salt, pepper to taste

Preheat oven to 350 degrees.

Trim ham slices of any fat and score edges.

In a small saucepan melt butter over medium-high heat. Add onion. Sauté until translucent, about 5 minutes. Add apple cider or juice, diced apples, sugar, mustard, and cloves. Season with salt and pepper. Cook over medium heat 5 minutes.

Place 1 ham slice in a shallow baking dish. Spoon half the onion-apple mixture over it, spreading evenly. Top with other ham slice and remaining mixture. Bake, covered, in preheated oven for 1 hour. Remove from dish and serve. 6 servings. (The dish can be partially made ahead and cooked just before serving.)

*Treaty Stone Limerick beside Thomond Bridge.*

# ❀ SCOTCH HAGGIS

*"Fair fa your honest sonsie face,
Great chieftain o' the
puddin-race!"*

Aye 'tis Scotland's treasured national dish, haggis, a much-maligned, unpretentious and decidedly earthy concoction that Robbie Burns salutes in the first lines of his satirical ode, "To a Haggis."
A richly flavored and ancient form of sausage made of sheep's innards, oatmeal, suet, and seasonings, all boiled in the animal's stomach paunch, it's a noble preparation that has long been the butt of tedious jokes. We've all heard the ridicule about the famous and curious haggis, called everything from a "boiled bagpipe" to a "giant tea bag." Scottish postcards depict it as a bizarre short-legged Highland animal hooked on a line or in flight. "First catch your haggis," a Scot will laughingly tell a visitor.

Although some persons think the name comes from the French *hachér*, to chop, it is believed to have derived from the Scottish word *hag*, meaning to hack. But its ancestry goes back to ancient Greece, and is said to be one of the oldest of our "pudding" sausages.

As devotees of haggis will boast, millions of Scots can't be wrong about their beloved culinary triumph. While served in Scotland in various forms for breakfast, lunch and dinner, it reaches regal heights around the world on Hogmanay (New Year's Eve), St. Andrew's Night, and especially the Burns Night supper on January 25th.

For the highlight of the ceremonial meal is, to the skirl of bagpipes, applause and cry of "Hail Great Chieftain," the arrival of the haggis on a silver platter as everyone joins in a Gaelic toast, *slainte*, or good health. Traditional accompaniments are "neeps an' tatties" (mashed turnips and potatoes) and many "wee nips" of whisky.

Once made in Scottish homes by a complicated old-fashioned process, haggis is now generally bought at the butcher's shop where it's sold like any other sausage. In America it can be purchased in cans and at some specialty food stores including those specializing in Scottish products. One Kansas City, Missouri, firm sells "Scotsfare Haggis Pups," or small sausages, made of lean pork and seasonings.

Two of my Scottish friends, Charles Marwick and his wife, Helen Lille, who live in Georgetown, D.C., serve a homemade steamed haggis made with lamb or veal liver, pinhead oats, suet or beef fat, minced onions and lamb, and gravy. 'Tis a bonny success at their social gatherings.

For pub or other parties, it's fun to offer small portions of haggis with a wee dram of whisky. Anyone who has not tasted haggis but has heard it described, typically approaches the dish timidly. But the surprise at the goodness of the fare is always a delight to me and all Scots. So here's to haggis!

Novices are advised not to undertake the making of a traditional haggis. In America it can be purchased in cans or from some specialty or Scottish food stores.

# Vegetables
# and
# Salads

*Ring of Kerry. Children playing an accordion and Irish whistle.*

*"The art of a country always has its roots in the soil, and the study of comparative cookery shows that however plentiful and varied the imported foodstuffs, it is the natural conditions and products that determine the general character of the national cuisines."*

— F. Marian McNeill

Although the Celts, and later the Gaels, had to rely on a limited choice of plants, roots, and herbs gathered or grown in their own particular area and eaten seasonally, they paid homage to their basic vegetables and salad greens by preparing them in innovative dishes.

From ancient times the Scots and Irish wisely utilized humble foods such as wild greens, seaweed, nettles, and members of the onion family—garlic, leeks, and scallions—for their daily fare. During winter, in the absence of greens, the roots of wild vegetables were cooked in basic dishes, providing variety to what was often a bland diet.

Gaels who lived near the rocky coasts of Scotland and Ireland also could gather a number of seaweeds which had pungent flavors, and were full of minerals and vitamins, relished centuries ago as health foods.

Fortunately, a great many of these culinary treasures are still enjoyed in Gaelic lands. Thus this selection of recipes is an interesting and different one.

## ❀ POTATOES

No single food is so closely associated with Ireland as the potato. "A day without potatoes is a day without nourishment," is an old saying. And a song, from the early 19th century, expresses the Irish sentiment about its beloved staple:

> *"Sublime potatoes! that from Antrim's shore*
> *To famous Kerry, from the poor man's store;*
> *Agreeing well with every place and state*
> *The peasant's noggin, or the rich man's plate."*

Ah, to be sure. The Irish have a flair for cooking and serving their *praties*, and from the moment one arrives in the country the potato appears to be in one form or another on virtually every menu and dining table.

Potatoes, said to have been introduced to Ireland from America in the late 16th century, have had more than a culinary connection with the country. For its social history is linked to that of the ubiquitous tuber. Some persons say that Irish nationalism was nourished on potatoes.

Certainly the vegetable kept the people alive during difficult times. For not only were potatoes easy to grow but they could be cooked quickly in the home three-legged pot, and then skinned, mashed, and flavored with butter and milk and a few seasonings to make nourishing meals. But over the years cooks also used the humble vegetable to make many creative dishes with imaginative names such as *champ*, *fadge*, and *boxty*.

It was the Irish dependence on this food that made the great potato famine of the 1840s such a disastrous and defining event in the country's modern history.

The Irish Famine Museum at Strokestown Park, Strokestown, in County Roscommon, housed in the stableyards of the sprawling mansion, documents in detail this calamity which reshaped Ireland's history, reducing the population by nearly three million people through starvation and mass emigration.

In the museum a range of exhibits in a series of interconnected rooms explains the cause of the famine: an over-reliance on a single kind of a cheap potato, which was vulnerable to the particular blight fungus that struck a country living almost entirely on this vegetable.

An immense cooking cauldron recalls the soup kitchens that were set up to feed the hungry people. And, appropriately, the museum houses a small restaurant where one of the specialties is a peasant soup, made with potatoes.

As in Ireland, the potato became a diet staple in Scotland where it took some time for it to be accepted as a food. But hungry crofters realized that the tuber could grow easily on their stony, peaty northern soil and, over the years, potatoes became the staff of life for countryfolk. Scots are partial to innovative dishes combining them with fish, oats, and other vegetables. And fortunately their potatoes have a special flavor and come in many colors as the country's climatic conditions are well suited to the cultivation of the tuber.

Here are a few of the traditional potato recipes.

## ❀ COLCANNON

*"Did you ever eat Colcannon*
*when 'twas made with yellow cream,*
*And the kale and praties blended*
*like the picture in a dream?*
*Did you ever take a forkful*
*and dip it in the lake*
*Of clover-flavored butter*
*that your mother used to make?"*

This old folk song honors colcannon, a treasured Gaelic mashed potato dish, as it used to be made from potatoes, kale, rich cream, and butter. Now the preferred green is cabbage. Once a a traditional harvest dish, it has long been a favorite Halloween specialty that includes a good luck symbol. The name is from three Gaelic words: *cal* (cabbage) and *ceann fionn* (white-headed). Although associated especially with Ireland, there is a Scottish Highland colcannon that includes carrots and/or turnips.

1 pound (about 3 medium) potatoes, peeled and halved
Salt
4 tablespoons unsalted butter, cut up
1 pound (about ½ head) green cabbage, shredded
½ cup hot milk
Freshly ground pepper
10 scallions, with some tops, cleaned and sliced
⅓ cup chopped fresh parsley
Additional 2 to 3 tablespoons unsalted butter, softened

In a medium heavy saucepan cover the potatoes with cold water. Add salt to taste. Bring to a boil over high heat. Reduce heat to medium-low and cook until potatoes are tender, about 20 minutes. With a slotted spoon, transfer from liquid to a large bowl. Add 2 tablespoons cut-up butter; mash until smooth and creamy.

Meanwhile, add the shredded cabbage to potato liquid in saucepan. Cook, covered, over medium-low heat until tender but crisp, about 7 minutes. Transfer cabbage to potato mixture. Add hot milk and remaining 2 tablespoons cut-up butter. Season with salt and pepper. Stir in scallions and parsley; mix well. (Prepare ahead up to this point and reheat, covered, in a 350-degree oven, if desired).

Serve mounded on a plate with a depression in the center. Fill with softened butter. Each forkful of the creamy mixture is dipped in the butter before eating. (A glass of buttermilk is the traditional accompaniment). 6 servings.

# ❀ BELFAST SCALLION MASHED POTATOES

Another traditional Irish mashed potato dish, eaten particularly in the northern counties, is called *champ*. Although generally flavored with scallions, it also can be made with leeks, chives, young nettles, or green peas. The following catchy rhyme was prompted by the wooden pestle or beetle used in homes to mash or pound large quantities of the cooked potatoes:

*"There was an old woman/ who lived in a lamp/ she had no room to beetle her champ./ She's up with her beetle/ and broke the lamp/ and then she had room to beetle her champ."*

A good place to enjoy *champ* is the atmospheric 19th century Crown Liquor Saloon on Great Victoria Street in Belfast, the city's best known pub. Now owned by the National Trust, it's famed for its long bar, ornate decor, and carved wooden snugs (cubicles), each with its own door and call bell, as well as fine traditional fare.

2 pounds (6 medium) all-purpose potatoes, peeled and quartered
Salt
½ cup (1 stick) unsalted butter, softened
About 1 cup milk or light cream
1 cup sliced scallions, with some pale green tops
Freshly ground pepper
About 3 tablespoons melted butter

In a medium heavy saucepan cover the potatoes with cold water. Add salt to taste. Bring to a boil over high heat. Reduce heat to medium-low and cook, covered, until tender, about 20 minutes. Drain. Return potatoes to pan. Place over low heat to allow any water from potatoes to evaporate. Place a clean kitchen towel across top of pan. Cover with lid. Remove from heat. Let stand 10 minutes. Add ¼ cup (½ stick) butter; mash well.

Meanwhile, in a small heavy saucepan, bring the milk or cream to a simmer. Add the scallions; simmer 5 minutes. Mix in remaining ¼ cup butter. Add to mashed potatoes. Season with salt and pepper.

Serve mounded on a plate with a depression in the center. Fill with melted butter. Each forkful of the creamy mixture is dipped in the butter before eating. 6 servings. (The dish can be prepared 2 to 3 hours ahead. Cover; let stand at room temperature. Rewarm over low heat, stirring frequently. Or, prepare ahead, cover with foil and reheat in a 350-degree oven.)

## ❀ PRATIE OATEN

In Malachie McCormick's charming booklet, *In Praise Of Irish Breakfasts*, he describes this Gaelic favorite as "A down-to-earth potato and oatmeal 'cake,' something similar to a potato pancake, and absolutely ideal for breakfast." True. But I also like to serve the cakes for pub parties as they are always winners.

2 cups warm stiff mashed potatoes
About 1 cup old-fashioned rolled oats
Salt, freshly ground pepper
About ½ cup (1 stick) unsalted butter, melted

In a medium bowl combine the mashed potatoes and ½ cup oats. Season with salt and pepper. Add 1 to 2 tablespoons melted butter, adding more oats if needed to make a firm but soft dough. Sprinkle a clean surface with oats. Turn out potato mixture on them. Roll out to a ½-inch thickness. With a floured 2½-inch biscuit cutter, cut into 12 rounds. Sprinkle tops with oats. Refrigerate, covered with plastic wrap, until ready to fry.

To cook, melt butter on a hot griddle or in a large skillet over medium-high heat. When hot, add the rounds. Fry, turning once, until golden on both sides, about 7 minutes. Serve hot with butter. Makes 12 cakes.

## ❀ FADGE

A flat, golden griddle or pan-fried potato cake, made in rounds or triangles, is part of Ireland's time-honored "Irish Fry," also called Ulster Fry. Once the hearty repast was served as an evening meal but now it is a traditional breakfast.

1½ pounds (6 medium) all-purpose potatoes, peeled and
    cut into large cubes
Salt
¼ cup milk
3 tablespoons unsalted butter, cut up
About 4 tablespoons all-purpose flour
2 tablespoons chopped fresh parsley
1 tablespoon chopped chives
Freshly ground pepper
2 tablespoons vegetable oil or butter
Melted butter

In a medium heavy saucepan cover the potatoes with cold water. Add salt to taste. Bring to a boil over high heat. Reduce heat to medium-low and cook, covered, until tender, about 12 minutes.

Drain. Transfer potatoes to a large bowl. While still warm, mash. Mix in flour, enough to make a stiff mixture. Turn out on a lightly floured board; knead lightly. Pat or roll into a ½-inch thick circle. Using a 3-inch biscuit cutter, cut out 8 cakes. (Place on a plate. Refrigerate, covered with plastic wrap, until ready to cook, up to 12 hours, if desired.)

To fry, heat oil or melt butter in a large skillet over medium-high heat. When hot, add potato cakes. Fry, turning once, until golden on both sides, about 5 minutes. Serve hot with melted butter. Makes 8 cakes.

## ❀ STOVIES WITH MUSHROOMS

To "stove" vegetables and/or other foods is a method of cooking in Scotland that means to cook slowly in an enclosed pot. It's a favorite way of cooking potatoes, either whole or sliced.

3 tablespoons unsalted butter
1 tablespoon vegetable oil
1 large onion, peeled and sliced thinly
2 pounds (about 12) small new potatoes, peeled
½ cup meat broth or water
Salt, freshly ground pepper
1 pound fresh mushrooms, cleaned and sliced thickly
⅓ cup chopped fresh dill or parsley
½ cup toasted oats (optional)

In a large saucepan melt the butter and heat the oil over medium-high heat. Add sliced onions; sauté until translucent, about 5 minutes. Add potatoes; sauté 5 minutes. Pour in broth or water. Season with salt and pepper. Reduce heat to medium-low.

Cook potatoes, covered, until just tender, about 25 minutes. Add mushrooms during last 10 minutes of cooking. Serve sprinkled with dill or parsley and, if desired, toasted oats. 6 servings.

## ❀ SCOTCH KALE AND OATS

*Kail*, as Scots call their dark green curly kale, is the national vegetable, grown in several varieties and used as a primary ingredient in a number of nourishing simple dishes. Generally boiled and seasoned with butter, it is often combined with oats or with mashed potatoes, onions, and milk as well as other vegetables.

At one time *kail* was an everyday term for a meal. "Will ye come and tak' your kail wi' me?" was an invitation for supper or dinner. Kail-time was supper-time.

This is a typical Highland recipe. It's a good accompaniment for meat or poultry.

¼ cup old-fashioned rolled oats
3 tablespoons unsalted butter
½ cup sliced scallions, with some pale green tops
2 pounds fresh kale, washed, stemmed and chopped
¾ cup meat or vegetable broth or water
Salt, freshly ground pepper
¼ cup light cream or milk

Spread oats in a medium ungreased skillet. Toast over medium-high heat, stirring 2 or 3 times, until edges are golden, about 3 minutes. Remove from heat; cool.

In a medium heavy saucepan melt butter over medium-high heat. Add scallions; sauté 2 minutes. Add kale leaves and broth or water. Season with salt and pepper. Cook, covered, stirring once or twice, until kale is tender, about 12 minutes. Add cream or milk. Serve sprinkled with toasted oats. 6 servings.

## ❀ SPICY RED CABBAGE WITH APPLES

Dating back to the time of the Celts, cabbage has been a favorite Gaelic vegetable. Both the green and red varieties are used extensively in Scottish and Irish cuisines. But the purplish-red kind is a favorite for holiday meals, served especially with game, pork or duck dishes. This dish is best if prepared the day before and reheated.

1 medium-head (about 2½ pounds) red cabbage
3 tablespoons unsalted butter
1 cup finely chopped yellow onions
2 tart cooking apples, peeled, cored, and chopped
½ cup red wine vinegar
2 tablespoons brown sugar
¼ teaspoon ground cinnamon
¼ teaspoon ground allspice
⅛ teaspoon ground cloves
Salt, freshly ground pepper
1 cup apple juice or cider

Wash and drain cabbage. Cut out and discard the tough core and remove any wilted outer leaves. With a sharp knife cut into shreds.

In a large, heavy saucepan melt the butter over medium-low heat. Add onion; sauté until translucent, about 5 minutes. Add shredded cabbage; sauté 4 minutes. Add chopped apple, vinegar, sugar, cinnamon, allspice, and cloves. Season with salt and pepper. Pour in apple juice or cider. Cook, covered, over medium-low heat until cabbage is tender and juices thicken slightly, about 1 hour. (Prepare beforehand. Refrigerate, covered, up to 3 days. Reheat slowly.) 8 servings.

## ❀ SCOTCH BASHED NEEPS

*Neep* is the Gaelic word for a disagreeable person and the turnip, a root vegetable also called rutabaga or Swede, that has an appealing sweet yellow flesh with a peppery taste. In Scotland it is a staple cold-weather vegetable, served bashed or mashed as a traditional accompaniment for haggis, and as tartan *purry* or purée, ginger-flavored mashed turnips. This dish combines mashed turnips and potatoes.

1 medium (about 2 pounds) rutabaga
Salt
1 pound (3 to 4 medium) potatoes, peeled and quartered
1 medium yellow onion, peeled and minced
2 tablespoons unsalted butter
3 tablespoons light cream or milk
2 teaspoons sugar
¼ teaspoon ground allspice
Freshly ground pepper

Scrub rutabaga and cut off the outer skin. Cut into cubes. In a medium heavy saucepan cook, covered, in 1 inch boiling salted water over medium-high heat for 30 minutes. Add potatoes and onion and continue cooking until vegetables are tender, about 20 minutes. Drain and mash. Mix in butter, cream or milk, sugar, and allspice. Season with salt and pepper. Serve warm. 4 to 6 servings.


## ✸ ORANGE-GLAZED CARROTS


The golden carrot, an excellent source of vitamin A, has been developed from an ancient weed to a vegetable of many varieties. In Ireland where it was known as "honey underground," the carrot figures in all sorts of dishes, from soups to sweet pies and puddings and cakes. This dish is made with baby carrots that are easy to cook and tasty.

2 tablespoons unsalted butter
3 tablespoons sliced scallions, with some pale green tops
1 16-ounce package peeled trimmed baby carrots, scrubbed
2 teaspoons honey
¾ cup orange juice
¼ teaspoon ground ginger
Salt, freshly ground pepper
2 tablespoons chopped fresh dill or parsley

In a medium skillet melt the butter over medium-high heat. Add scallions; sauté 1 minute. Remove to a dish. Add carrots to the drippings. Sauté until they begin to brown slightly, about 8 minutes. Add honey and orange juice. Bring to a boil. Reduce heat to medium-low. Add ginger. Season with salt and pepper. Simmer until liquid is reduced to a glaze, stirring occasionally, and carrots are tender, about 15 minutes. Add scallions; mix well. Transfer to a serving dish. Serve sprinkled with dill or parsley. 4 to 6 servings.

# ❀ NETTLES

Nettles, a number of related weeds with stinging hairs that have to be picked and prepared with gloves on, are highly prized in Scotland and Ireland, where they are eaten as a green, either plain or topped with poached eggs, or used to flavor potato and oatmeal dishes and beer, and to make soups. Rich in iron and vitamins, nettles have a spinachlike flavor. In the spring, when they are young and tender, the Scots and Irish drink quantities of nettle tea or broth to ensure good health the rest of the year. It is said to have been a favorite of St. Columba. In James Joyce's *Lives of the Saints*, he gives the story of the saint and nettle soup made with oatmeal.

If you have nettles, cook them like spinach in a little broth, and season with butter, salt and pepper.

# ❀ SEA VEGETABLES

Seaweed, or sea vegetables, as the many different varieties are sometimes known, has been an important staple in the Scottish and Irish diets since prehistoric times. Found all along the lengthy coasts, it was used in many ways, including cookery and the flavoring of drinks. The Gaels inherited a vast knowledge about these plants from the Celts who valued them not only as foods but for important medicinal purposes. For seaweed is one of nature's richest sources of vegetable protein, vitamin B-12, and vital trace minerals.

Among the best known of the seaweeds, gathered particularly in April and May, washed and left to bleach in the sun, is carrageen or carragheen, also called Irish moss or sea moss. The name comes from the Gaelic *carraig*, meaning rock. Either dark purple or green, it can be eaten fresh but the seaweed is usually purchased dried. When reconstituted in a liquid it releases a gelatinous substance that is added to drinks, soups, jellies, creams, and puddings. Sweetened carrageen, or moss pudding, is a traditional Gaelic dessert. Because of its very high vitamin content, carrageen is a popular health food, and, in recent years, has been acclaimed by a number of American and Irish chefs who are adding it to a variety of interesting dishes, from condiments to desserts.

Dulse, also called dillisk, is a dark reddish purple seaweed with a pungent briny taste that imparts a pleasing taste of the sea to many culinary preparations. Usually sold dried, the leaves can be chewed or used to enhance drinks, soups, and seafood or vegetable, especially potato, dishes.

Ballycastle, a resort town in County Antrim, where the Atlantic Ocean meets the Irish Sea, stages an annual Auld or Oul" Lammas Fair, a modern version of the ancient Celtic harvest festival, Lughnasa, in late August. One of Ireland's oldest fairs, dating back to 1606, it features two unusual foods: yellowman, a hard, very sticky, yellow toffee, and dulse, sold heavily salted and ready to eat.

Sloke, known in Wales as laver, and also called sea spinach as it is cooked like the vegetable, is a leafy green seaweed that is sold fresh. It goes well with mashed potatoes.

## ❀ SEA KALE

Several kinds of sea kale, a nutritious herb of the mustard family, is a renowned spring delicacy gathered along some Gaelic coasts. Cooked and served simply like asparagus, the kale is also highly prized for salads. The tender young curly grayish-green or blue-green leaves are sold either bleached or unbleached. When washed and dried, they may be simply tossed with a vinaigrette dressing, or combined with chopped chives and tarragon leaves and a mustard-flavored oil-vinegar dressing.

## ❀ WATERCRESS-EGG SALAD

The noted Irish writer Theodora Fitzgibbon recorded that the tiny-leafed, dark green plant called watercress or cress, is frequently mentioned in early books and was listed among the "curious salads" eaten by the Irish. Watercress is still grown all over Ireland and enjoyed as an ingredient for tea sandwiches as well as in soups and salads. Not only does the colorful green have an appealing, peppery flavor, but it is also valued for its high calcium and vitamins A and C content.

2 bunches watercress
½ cup sliced scallions, with some pale green tops
2 hard-cooked eggs, shelled and sliced
3 to 4 tablespoons olive oil
1 tablespoon wine vinegar
Salt, freshly ground pepper
2 medium ripe red tomatoes, peeled and cut into wedges

Wash watercress well; cut leaves from stems, discarding any wilted ones. Drain or spin dry. Refrigerate until ready to use.

To prepare, place watercress leaves in a salad bowl. Add scallions; toss. Place sliced eggs over leaves. In a small dish combine the oil and vinegar. Season with salt and pepper. Pour over salad ingredients. Toss lightly. Serve at once, garnished with tomato wedges. 4 to 6 servings.

# ❀ SCOTTISH SYBOE SALAD

Scots are fond of a colorful salad made with sliced tomatoes and scallions or *syboes*, a word derived from the French *ciboule*, small onion. The salad is a good accompaniment for cold roast meat or poultry.

4 large ripe red tomatoes, peeled and sliced
1 cup sliced scallions, with some pale green tops
3 tablespoons olive or vegetable oil
1 tablespoon cider vinegar
1 teaspoon sugar
Salt, freshly ground pepper
Fresh watercress leaves

Arrange tomato slices, overlapping, in a serving dish. Sprinkle with scallions. In a small jar combine the oil, vinegar, and sugar. Pour over the tomatoes and scallions. Season with salt and pepper. Let stand at room temperature 30 minutes before serving. Garnish with watercress leaves. 6 servings.

# ❀ BEET-APPLE SALAD

Gaels favor the deep red roots of beets in sweet-sour sauces, pickled, and in salads. In this appealing specialty the beets are combined with apples and piquant flavorings.

1 can (1 pound) small beets, drained and sliced or chopped
½ cup minced onions
2 medium tart apples, peeled, cored and diced
3 tablespoons wine vinegar
2 teaspoons prepared horseradish, drained
2 teaspoons sugar
Salt, freshly ground pepper

In a medium bowl combine the beets, onions, and apples. In a small dish mix the vinegar, horseradish, and sugar. Pour over the beet-apple mixture. Season with salt and pepper. Refrigerate, covered, up to 8 hours, to blend flavors. 4 to 6 servings.

## ❀ IRISH TOSSED DANDELION SALAD

The common dandelion, a name derived from the French *dent de lion* or lion's tooth, for its sharply indented leaves, is a favorite Gaelic food. Young tender greens, freshly picked, were once welcome spring greens, treasured for their bitter taste, and storehouse of nutrients. They were also considered a valuable spring tonic. Now they are in fashion again, used primarily alone or mixed with other greens in salads.

In Gaelic lore the dandelion was sacred to the goddess Brigit, and the yellow dandelion blossom is called "Brigit's, or Bridget's Flower."

1 pound small, tender dandelion leaves
2 cups chopped, cleaned celery
½ cup grated, scraped carrots
1 small yellow or white onion, peeled and minced
About ½ cup sour cream
2 tablespoons fresh lemon juice
Salt, freshly ground pepper
2 tablespoons chopped fresh dill
1 large ripe red tomato, peeled and cut into wedges

Wash and dry dandelion leaves. Cut off roots and discard any bruised leaves; tear into 2-inch pieces. Refrigerate until ready to serve.

In a large salad bowl combine the dandelion leaves, celery, carrots, and onions. In a small bowl whisk the sour cream and lemon juice. Season with salt and pepper. Pour over salad; toss to combine. Add dill and tomato wedges. Toss again. Serve at once. 4 servings.

# ❀ CREAMY BUTTERMILK COLESLAW

The utilitarian and familiar cabbage, so beloved by the Gaels, is crammed with vitamins and available in several varieties. Celts were among the first to cultivate the sturdy plant which is now used to make a good many country dishes, including coleslaws. Buttermilk imparts an appealing tangy flavor to this one.

4 cups finely shredded green cabbage
1 tablespoon sugar
½ cup minced onions
1 cup finely chopped green peppers
½ teaspoon dried dillweed
Salt, freshly ground pepper
1 cup buttermilk
1 tablespoon fresh lemon juice
½ teaspoon Dijon-style mustard

Place shredded cabbage in a large bowl. Sprinkle with sugar; toss to mix well. Refrigerate, covered, 30 minutes. Add onions, green peppers, and dillweed. Season with salt and pepper.

In a small dish whisk buttermilk, lemon juice, and mustard. Season with salt and pepper. Pour over cabbage mixture. Toss to mix well. Refrigerate, covered, 3 hours or overnight. Mix again before serving. 6 to 8 servings.

# ❀ PUB POTATO SALAD

A well-flavored potato salad is a traditional pub specialty and holds a place of honor at outdoor meals. Here's one of my favorites to serve on any occasion.

4 medium all-purpose potatoes, scrubbed
Salt
1¼ cups sour cream at room temperature
2 tablespoons wine vinegar
½ teaspoon dried dillweed
Freshly ground pepper
½ cup diced green pepper
½ cup diced celery
½ cup sliced scallions, with some pale green tops
3 hard-cooked eggs, shelled and chopped
¼ teaspoon paprika
1 large ripe red tomato, peeled and cut into wedges

In a large heavy saucepan cook potatoes in their jackets in a little salted boiling water until tender, about 25 minutes. Drain well; peel. While still warm, cut into cubes into a medium bowl. Add sour cream, vinegar, and dillweed. Season with salt and pepper. Add green pepper, celery, scallions, and eggs; mix well. Leave at room temperature for 1 hour to blend flavors before serving. Or refrigerate, covered, up to 4 hours. Serve sprinkled with paprika and garnished with tomato wedges. 6 servings.

# ❀ ST. PATRICK'S "SHAMROCK" SALAD

*St. Patrick's "Chosen leaf*
*Of bard and chief,*
*Old Erin's native Shamrock."*

The shamrock, *Seamrog* in Gaelic, is a humble three-leafed plant resembling clover that grows wild all over Ireland and has a prominent place in the country's history.

According to Gaelic lore it is St. Patrick who was responsible for the shamrock becoming the national Irish emblem in the course of his preaching. When his listeners were unable to comprehend the Holy Trinity as a unity, he is said to have plucked a shamrock from the ground and asked, "Is it not as possible for the Father, the Son and the Holy Ghost, as for these three leaves to grow upon a single stalk?" The doubters found this logic unassailable.

Long ago the name "shamrock" meant various wild greens, not just the famous trefoil. Now in Ireland a "shamrock" salad is made with a mixture of fresh greens such as dulse, watercress, sorrel, burnet, or whatever grows in the garden. This salad is flavored with garlic, another favorite Irish food that has been known and eaten in Ireland since ancient times.

1 garlic clove, peeled and minced or crushed
Salt
1 to 2 tablespoons wine vinegar
½ teaspoon dry mustard
5 to 6 tablespoons olive oil
Freshly ground pepper
2 quarts mixed salad greens, washed, dried, torn into
     bite-sized pieces, and chilled

In a salad bowl combine the garlic, salt to taste, vinegar, and mustard. Crush with a pestle or back of a spoon. Gradually add oil; season with pepper. Blend with a whisk or fork. Add greens; toss to combine well. Serve at once. 4 to 6 servings.

# Breads

*Brodick Castle, Isle of Arran, Scotland.*

*"If every Frenchwoman is born with a wooden spoon in her hand, every Scotswoman is born with a rolling-pin under her arm."*

— F. Marian McNeill

*"The great variety of Irish breads owes its existence to the traditional eating habits of our people."*

— Monica Sheridan

Bannocks, baps, brunnies, butteries, oatcakes, parkins, pikelets, scones, shortbreads, singing hinnies, and softies. On a recent trip, I wandered down the main street of Inverness, a royal burgh, capital of the Scottish Highlands, and site of Stone of the Tubs, known as "Clachnacudainn," where centuries ago women rested their washtubs, and early kings were crowned. History beckoned but bakeries won. It was impossible to resist the captivating window displays and omnipresent aromas drifting through the doors enticing passersby to sample the inviting array of breads with intriguing names.

So, on a sunny Saturday morning, I join the local shoppers for a refreshing cup of tea and to fill my tote bag with slices, loaves, and pieces, more than enough treats for lunch, my train journey north, and evening snacks.

From the moment I arrived in Scotland and Ireland I took great pleasure in sampling the delectable, traditional breads made in such variety that one can think of them as fantasy and fun as well as something good to eat.

One of the great traditions of Gaelic cooking is the excellence of its breads, and homemakers take enormous pride in baking for their family and friends. Bread has long been "the staff of life," playing a significant role in the history, religion, literature, and culture. And, until modern times, it came to the table, freshly baked and straight from the hearth.

The Celtic contribution to baking was considerable. As previously mentioned, Celts grew grains, invented a hand quern for grinding them, and had sieves. Their use of beer *barm* as a leavening agent resulted in lighter breads, and an early step towards oven-baking was taken when cooks put an inverted pot over the flat cakes as they baked.

Typical Gaelic bread originated as an unleavened round, flat cake that was cooked on a bakestone and later on a "girdle" or griddle, one of the world's oldest cooking utensils that was introduced by the early Celts. The bread was called bannock, a word that comes from the Gaelic *bonnach* which means cake. In ancient times it was made of barley or oats, although pease meal and powdered silverweed were also used. Later, wheat flour became the norm for luxury loaves.

Treasured fare for centuries, there are many customs and superstitions associated with bannocks. A number of them had symbolic or religious significance and were served at festivals and rites. A circle scalloped around the edges represented the sun. For the old celebration of Beltaine or May Day, the Druids made a flat barley cake, spiced with burnt heather and mistletoe pollen that was seared before it was broken into pieces and eaten.

There was a bannock for the festival of Imbolc (February 1st), and one for Midsummer Day, June 24, and Lughnasa, a joyous August celebration, as well as a Yule bannock, a Halloween bannock, and even a sweet "cryin" bannock served to women who assisted at an infant's birth. And, when a baby started to cut teeth, he or she was given a "teethin" oatmeal bannock baked with a ring inside it.

Over the years Gaels created a wide variety of bannocks. Although the early forms were made without raising agents, cooks later added a leavening to the meal or flour. Now they range from thin rough-textured ones that are cooked on a griddle to substantial, large kinds baked in the oven. Some special varieties are enriched with eggs, butter, a sweetener, fruit, or nuts.

Included here are recipes for a few bannocks and other Gaelic breads.

## ✸ CAPE BRETON AFTERNOON TEA BANNOCK

At my Aunt Annie's Vermont home it was always time for tea—upon rising, for breakfast, at eleven, in midafternoon, before retiring, and whenever a visitor dropped in. A guest at the doorstep was but another excuse for brewing a fresh pot of that warming beverage so beloved by the Scots. With the cups of strong tea my aunt served her favorite breads, especially this mildly sweet, soft and relatively thick bannock from her Cape Breton homeland.

2 cups all-purpose flour
1 cup old-fashioned rolled oats
⅓ cup light brown sugar
1 tablespoon baking powder
½ teaspoon baking soda
¾ teaspoon salt
½ cup (1 stick) unsalted butter, cold and diced
1 large egg, beaten
About ⅔ cup buttermilk
2 tablespoons unsalted butter, melted for topping

Preheat oven to 400 degrees. Lightly flour the center of a baking sheet.

In a large bowl combine the flour, oats, sugar, baking powder, baking soda, and salt. With a pastry blender, cut in ½ cup butter until mixture is uniformly crumbly.

In a small bowl whisk the egg and ⅔ cup buttermilk. Add to dry ingredients, stirring, until well blended to make a soft and moist dough, adding more buttermilk, if needed. Gather to form a ball. Place in center of prepared baking sheet. With floured hands, shape into a 10-inch round about ½-inch thick. Bake in preheated oven until evenly browned and a tester inserted into center comes out clean, about 18 minutes. Remove to a wire rack. While still warm, brush the top with melted butter. Serve warm or at room temperature, cut into wedges, with butter and marmalade. Makes 1 round loaf. 8 to 10 servings.

## ❊ HEBRIDEAN HARVEST BANNOCK

In the Hebridean Islands, *Struan Michel* or St. Michael's Bannock, a traditional large round bread was made of a mixture of several grains for the September harvest feast called Michaelmas. This is an adaptation that includes whole-wheat flour and cornmeal.

1 cup whole-wheat flour
1 cup yellow cornmeal
2 tablespoons light brown sugar
1 tablespoon baking soda
¾ teaspoon salt
3 tablespoons solid vegetable shortening
1 cup buttermilk

Preheat oven to 400 degrees. Lightly flour the center of a baking sheet.

In a large bowl combine the flour, cornmeal, sugar, baking soda, and salt. With a pastry blender, cut in shortening until mixture is uniformly crumbly. Gradually add buttermilk, stirring, until dry ingredients are moistened. Gather into a ball.

Place in center of prepared baking sheet. With floured hands, shape into an 8-inch round about ½-inch thick. With a floured sharp knife, cut a large deep cross on top of loaf.

Bake in preheated oven until evenly golden and tester inserted into center comes out clean, about 35 minutes. Remove to a wire rack. Serve warm, or at room temperature, cut into wedges, with butter and honey. Makes 1 round loaf. 8 to 10 servings.

## ❀ OATEN BANNOCK TRIANGLES

This is a crunchy raisin-studded bannock that is cut into triangles before baking.

1 cup whole-wheat flour
½ cup all-purpose flour
1 tablespoon baking powder
¾ teaspoon salt
1 cup old-fashioned rolled oats
2 tablespoons light brown sugar
¼ cup (½ stick) unsalted butter, cold and diced
½ cup raisins
¾ cup milk
Additional 3 tablespoons rolled oats

Preheat oven to 425 degrees. Lightly flour the center of a baking sheet.

In a large bowl combine the whole-wheat and all-purpose flours, baking powder, salt, 1 cup oats, and sugar. With a pastry blender, cut in butter until mixture is uniformly crumbly. Stir in raisins. Gradually add milk, stirring until well blended to make a soft and moist dough. Gather to form a ball.

Place in center of prepared baking sheet. With floured hands, shape into an 8-inch round about 1-inch thick. Sprinkle the top with additional 3 tablespoons oats, pressing lightly into dough. With a floured sharp knife, cut into 8 triangles. Do not separate.

Bake in preheated oven until evenly golden and tester inserted into center comes out clean, about 15 minutes. Remove to a wire rack. Serve warm or slightly cooled, separated into triangles, with butter and honey or marmalade. Makes 8.

## ❀ BRODICK SWEET BANNOCK

This mildly sweet bannock is named for Brodick Castle, the historic home of the dukes of Hamilton on the lovely southern Hebridean island of Arran. A property of the National Trust for Scotland, the castle is famed for its magnificent gardens and has an engaging basement kitchen with a superb collection of cooking equipment that includes a bread oven, bread boards, and other implements for making breads.

1 cup old-fashioned rolled oats
1 cup whole-wheat flour
1 tablespoon baking powder
3 tablespoons sugar
¾ teaspoon salt
¼ cup (½ stick) unsalted butter, cold and diced
1 large egg
3 to 4 tablespoons milk

Preheat oven to 375 degrees. Lightly flour the center of a baking sheet.

In a blender or food processor, with metal blade in place, process oats until ground to a fine texture.

In a large bowl combine the flour, baking powder, sugar, and salt. Stir in ground oats. With a pastry blender, cut in butter until mixture is uniformly crumbly. In a small bowl whisk the egg and 3 tablespoons milk. Add to dry ingredients, stirring to make a moist and soft dough, adding a little more milk, if needed. Gather to form a ball. Place in center of prepared baking sheet. With floured hands, shape into a 7- or 8-inch round about ½-inch thick. Bake in preheated oven until evenly golden and tester inserted into center comes out clean, about 20 minutes. Remove to a wire rack. Serve warm or at room temperature, cut into wedges, with butter and jam or marmalade. Makes 1 round loaf. 8 to 10 servings.

## ❀ OATCAKES

A crunchy, biscuit-like roundel with an appealing nutty taste, the oatcake is a treasured Celtic bread made now in many varieties. Although long enjoyed in Ireland, the cake is associated especially with Scotland. When Robbie Burns called his beloved Scotland the "Land o' Cakes," he meant the humble oatcake. "Oatmeal cakes and oatmeal porridge have made Scotchmen," is a common saying.

Early Scots survived on a frugal diet that included oatcakes, often prepared under primitive conditions. Shepherds and drovers mixed their oatmeal, carried in "great wallets" hung round their sturdy backs, with water and baked the flat cakes on hot stones. Fishermen in the Hebridean Islands sustained themselves with uncooked oatcakes made by moistening handfuls of oatmeal with sea water. On the island of Scarp, off the west coast of Harris, a "bonnach boise," or palm oatcake, was shaped between the palms of the hand, and toasted and turned in front of a glowing peat fire, propped up by a smooth slab of stone.

The ancient chronicler, Froissart, wrote that most 14th century soldiers carried a flat metal plate and a wallet of oatmeal. Using a little water, they were always able to make themselves oatcakes over an open fire.

Now there are many varieties of oatcakes that are wonderfully versatile. Although made from a few simple ingredients, the traditional wafer-thin oatcake that includes fine oatmeal, a little hot fat and water, plus a pinch of salt, is difficult to prepare. As I discovered, it takes a lot of practice and patience. Thus, many cooks prefer those that include flour, a leavening agent, and, perhaps sugar. Here's one of my family recipes.

## ✸ SHAW'S OATCAKES

I call these party oatcakes as my family recipe makes a large number that can be prepared ahead and stored until ready to serve.

1½ cups old-fashioned rolled oats
1½ cups all-purpose flour
½ cup sugar
½ teaspoon baking powder
½ teaspoon salt
¾ cup vegetable shortening
About ⅓ cup cold water

Preheat oven to 350 degrees.

Lightly grease 2 baking sheets.

In a large bowl thoroughly combine the oats, flour, sugar, baking powder, and salt. With a pastry blender, cut in shortening. Gradually add cold water, enough to make a stiff but pliable dough. Gather to form a ball.

Place dough on a lightly floured flat surface. Divide into 2 parts. With a floured rolling pin, roll each part into an 8-inch square with a ⅛-inch thickness. With a floured knife, cut each square into 16 2-inch squares. Transfer to prepared baking sheets. Bake in preheated oven until oatcakes are dry and firm, about 15 minutes. Transfer to wire racks. Serve warm, or cool and store in an airtight container. Makes about 2½ dozen.

## ❈ SCONES

Scones, delectable rich and crumbly biscuit-like cakes, enjoyed for breakfast, with afternoon tea, or as snacks, are treasured Gaelic breads that originated in Scotland. Now made in great variety, they are best served freshly cooked and warm with butter and marmalade or jam.

Pronounced "skonn," (to rhyme with on), the word's origin is uncertain. It may be from Middle Dutch *schoonbrot* (fine bread), Gaelic *sgoon* (block) or *sgoon aram* (block of bread). Some Scots believe the name came from Scone, a parish where Scottish kings were once crowned on the famed "stone of destiny."

Nothing about the scone resembles a stone. The bread is very soft and light, differing considerably from the original thin oatmeal or wheaten and sour cream cakes. Although scones are cut into various shapes, the traditional one is made in a small triangle, or "farl," cut from a round of dough before baking. While most scones are now baked, some, called drop scones, may be cooked on a griddle or in a heavy skillet almost like a pancake.

## ❀ CREAM SCONES

This is a basic recipe for a scone that can be served split, spread with butter and jam, and slathered with clotted cream for afternoon tea or breakfast, or another meal.

2 cups all-purpose flour
1 tablespoon baking powder
½ teaspoon salt
2 tablespoons sugar
¼ cup (½ stick) unsalted butter, cold and diced
1 large egg
About ½ cup light cream
Milk, butter and sugar for topping

Preheat oven to 425 degrees.

In a large bowl combine the flour, baking powder, salt, and sugar. With a pastry blender, cut in butter until mixture is uniformly crumbly.

In a small dish whisk the egg and ½ cup cream. Add to flour-butter mixture. Stir quickly and briefly to make a soft and sticky dough, adding a little more cream, if needed. Gather into a ball. Place on a lightly floured surface. With floured hands, knead gently. Roll into a circle to a ½-inch thickness. With a floured 2½-inch round cutter, cut into rounds, leaving as little dough as possible for rerolling. Place on an ungreased baking sheet, about 1 inch apart. Brush tops lightly with milk.

180

Bake in preheated oven until golden and puffed, about 12 minutes. Remove to a wire rack. Brush tops with butter and sprinkle with sugar. Allow to cool slightly, about 5 minutes. Serve warm or at room temperature. Makes 12 rounds.

## ❋ PARSLEY SCONE TRIANGLES

Use these colorful triangles for sandwiches, if desired. Split and fill with slivers of ham, beef, or other ingredients.

2¼ cups all-purpose flour
1 tablespoon baking powder
½ teaspoon baking soda
1 tablespoon sugar
¾ teaspoon salt
¼ cup (½ stick) unsalted butter, cold and diced
¾ cup chopped fresh parsley, washed and dried
1 teaspoon dried oregano
1 large egg
About ¾ cup buttermilk

Preheat oven to 400 degrees. Lightly butter a 10-inch round baking dish.

In a large bowl combine the flour, baking powder, baking soda, sugar, and salt. With a pastry blender, cut in butter until mixture is uniformly crumbly. Stir in parsley and oregano.

In a small dish whisk the egg, reserving 1 tablespoon of it, and ¾ cup buttermilk. Add to flour-butter mixture. Stir quickly and briefly to make a soft and sticky dough, adding more buttermilk, if needed. Gather into a ball.

Place on a lightly floured flat surface. With floured hands, knead gently. Roll into a circle to a ¾-inch thickness. Transfer to prepared dish; press gently to form an even round. Brush the top with reserved egg. With a sharp knife, cut into 8 equal triangles.

Bake in preheated oven until golden and puffed, about 25 minutes. Remove to a wire rack. Cool in dish 10 minutes. Cut again into 8 triangles. Serve warm. Makes 8.

## ❀ DILLED CHEESE SCONES

These are flavorful small scones that are ideal for parties.

2 cups all-purpose flour
2 teaspoons baking powder
½ teaspoon baking soda
½ teaspoon salt
¼ cup (½ stick) unsalted butter, cold and diced
1 cup grated Cheddar cheese
1 teaspoon dried dillweed
1 large egg
About ⅔ cup milk

EGG WASH:
1 egg mixed with 1 teaspoon water

Preheat oven to 425 degrees.

In a large bowl combine the flour, baking powder, baking soda, and salt. With a pastry blender, cut in butter until mixture is uniformly crumbly. Stir in cheese and dillweed; mix well.

In a small dish whisk the egg and ⅔ cup milk. Add to flour-butter mixture. Stir quickly and briefly to make a soft and sticky dough, adding a little more milk, if needed. Gather into a ball.

Place on a lightly floured surface. With floured hands, knead gently. Roll into a circle to a ½-inch thickness. With a floured cutter, cut into 2-inch rounds, leaving as little dough as possible for rerolling. Place on an ungreased baking sheet, about 1 inch apart. Brush tops lightly with egg wash.

Bake in preheated oven until golden and puffed, about 12 minutes. Remove to a wire rack. Cool slightly. Serve warm or at room temperature. Makes about 18.

## ✿ SODA BREAD

Like many Irishmen, Sean O'Casey, the famous dramatist, had fond childhood memories of soda bread, a very old form of food strongly associated with Ireland. "Underneath a deep deep drawer, going the whole length of the cart, filled with lovely white an' brown squares, soda squares, currant squares, and brown loaves, covered with their shining golden crust. . . ," he wrote in *The Street Sings* about the breads that sold for tuppence in street vans.

Soda bread, once baked on peat fires in a three-legged iron pot called a *bastable* oven, is a joy to prepare and serve. It requires only a few ingredients, is easy to put together, and takes little time to bake. The bread makes marvelous breakfast toast, often is served for tea, and is ideal for informal dining. Like any old favorite, soda bread comes in many forms: white, brown, sweet, made with caraway seeds and currants, and flavored with honey or molasses-like treacle.

When mixed and shaped into a circular loaf, the bread is marked with an X or cross on the top. Some Irish cooks believe that this signifies a religious blessing to ensure good bread; others say the cross scares away the devil. Perhaps it's done to prevent the loaf from cracking irregularly. Treasured for it's pleasing, distinctive taste, soda bread is best served the day it is baked as it dries out quickly. Slice and toast on the second day, if desired.

Here are two of my favorite recipes for soda bread.

## ❀ KERRY BROWN SODA BREAD

The Ring of Kerry, Ireland's famous 110-mile scenic drive, a glorious panorama of seacoast, mountain, and lakeland vistas, is also an outpost of Gaelic culture. There are outdoor attractions and natural spectacles galore but one of the great delights is to stop at a café, tea shop, or bakery for some wonderfully aromatic soda bread. This is my version of a loaf I enjoyed in Trallee, a lovely town that celebrates with an annual Rose of Trallee festival.

2 cups whole-wheat flour
1 cup all-purpose flour
2 teaspoons sugar
1½ teaspoons baking powder
½ teaspoon baking soda
1 teaspoon salt
2 tablespoons unsalted butter, cold and diced
1¼ cups buttermilk

Preheat oven to 375 degrees. Lightly butter the center of a baking sheet.

In a large bowl combine the whole-wheat and all-purpose flours, sugar, baking powder, baking soda, and salt. With a pastry blender, cut in butter until mixture is uniformly crumbly. Make a well in center of dry ingredients. Gradually pour in buttermilk, stirring only until dry ingredients are moistened. Gather into a ball.

Place on a lightly floured surface. With floured hands, knead lightly and quickly until smooth. Shape into a ball. Place in center of prepared baking sheet. Form into an 8-inch round with a slightly raised center. With a floured sharp knife, cut a large deep cross on top of loaf.

Bake in preheated oven until loaf is golden brown and sounds hollow when tapped on the bottom, about 40 minutes. Remove to a wire rack. Cool slightly. Cut into wedges and serve warm. Makes 1 loaf. 8 servings.

*Bakers' Shop, Isle of Arran. That car wouldn't get out of my way in front of the bakery.*

# ❀ CURRANT SODA BREAD

This soda bread is flavored with the sweetness of currants, once known as the "raisins of Corinth" which became a favorite Gaelic addition to breads and cakes.

2 cups all-purpose flour
2 tablespoons sugar
1½ teaspoons baking powder
½ teaspoon baking soda
½ teaspoon salt
3 tablespoons unsalted butter, cold and diced
½ cup dried currants
About ¾ cup buttermilk
1 tablespoon melted unsalted butter

Preheat oven to 375 degrees. Lightly butter the center of a baking sheet.

In a large bowl combine the flour, sugar, baking powder, baking soda, and salt. With a pastry blender, cut in butter until mixture is uniformly crumbly. Mix in currants. Make a well in center of dry ingredients. Gradually pour in buttermilk, enough to make a soft dough, stirring only until dry ingredients are moistened. Gather into a ball.

Place on a lightly floured flat surface. With floured hands, knead lightly and quickly until smooth. Shape into a ball. Place on prepared baking sheet. With floured hands, shape into a 7-inch round with a slightly raised center. With a floured sharp knife, cut a large deep cross on top of loaf.

Bake in preheated oven until loaf is golden brown and sounds hollow when tapped on the bottom, about 35 minutes. Remove to a wire rack. Brush top with melted butter. Cool. Cut into wedges and serve slightly warm. Makes 1 loaf. 8 servings.

# ❀ BOXTY

*"Boxty on the griddle, Boxty in the pan/*
*If you don't get Boxty, you'll never get a man."*

As the rhyme says, there are two kinds of this Northern Ireland specialty. Boxty on the griddle is like a pancake; in the pan it resembles a bread. Made initially in the counties of Donegal, Leitrim and Covan, boxty is a traditional dish for St. Bridget's Day and All Hallows Eve, Halloween, when a ring wrapped in wax paper is mixed with the batter. The lucky girl who finds it is destined to be wed.

Old-timers say that the name dates back to the days when homes didn't have a commercial grater, and a substitute was made by punching holes into a box or flattened tin can.

A great place to enjoy this specialty is Gallagher's Boxty House near Trinity College in Dublin's Old City. Here there's lilting Irish music and festive fare, including boxty made as a potato pancake rolled thin, grilled, and with a choice of chicken, lamb, beef, fish, or vegetable filling.

1 cup shredded raw peeled potatoes*
1 cup mashed cooked potatoes*
1 cup all-purpose flour
1 teaspoon baking powder
1 teaspoon salt
1 tablespoon unsalted butter, melted
About ¼ cup sour cream or milk
Freshly ground white or black pepper
Vegetable oil and butter for frying
Additional melted butter
*For the grated and mashed potatoes you will need 6 to 7 medium all-purpose potatoes.

Place raw potatoes on a piece of cheesecloth or tea towel; squeeze to remove all liquid. Turn potatoes into a large bowl. Add mashed potatoes; mix well. Sift in flour, baking powder, and salt; mix well. Add 1 tablespoon melted butter and sour cream or milk, enough to make a firm but pliable dough.

Turn dough onto a lightly floured surface; knead lightly. Pat or roll out to a circle about ½-inch thick. With a floured biscuit cutter, cut out 8 cakes. (Place on a plate; cover with plastic wrap; refrigerate until 30 minutes before frying, up to 8 hours or overnight.)

To fry the boxty: In a large skillet, heat the oil, with or without a little butter, over medium-hot heat. Add the cakes and fry 5 minutes, turning once, until golden on both sides. Serve hot topped with melted butter. Makes 8.

## ❀ LEMON-WALNUT TEA BREAD

The Scots and Irish make an interesting repertoire of savory quick breads that closely resemble cakes in flavor and texture, and are served with afternoon tea. Usually a little sweet, many of the tea breads are enhanced with nuts, raisins, or fruit. Although excellent when served warm, the flavors will mature if the bread is stored a day or two. This delicately flavored loaf is both tart and sweet.

1 large lemon
½ cup (1 stick) unsalted butter, softened
1 cup sugar
2 large eggs
1½ cups all-purpose flour
1½ teaspoons baking powder
1 teaspoon salt
½ cup chopped walnuts
½ cup milk or light cream
Confectioners' sugar

Preheat oven to 350 degrees. Lightly butter and flour the bottom and sides of a 9 × 5 × 3-inch loaf pan.

Peel or grate 2 tablespoons of lemon rind. Squeeze and reserve 2 tablespoons of the juice.

In a large bowl cream the butter and sugar until light and fluffy. Mix in lemon rind. Add eggs, one at a time; beat well.

Into a medium bowl sift together the flour, baking powder and salt. Mix in walnuts. Add to butter-sugar mixture alternately with milk or cream and lemon juice, beating until well blended. Turn batter into prepared pan.

Bake in preheated oven until loaf is golden and tester inserted into center comes out clean. Cool in pan 10 minutes. Remove from pan to a wire rack. Cool slightly and serve warm. Or, cool; wrap in foil; let stand overnight in cool, dry place for 1 to 2 days. Serve the bread cut in thin slices. Makes 1 loaf. 10 to 12 servings.

# ❀ SLIGO TEA BUNS

Although William Butler Yeats, Ireland's most celebrated poet, and a dramatist and essayist, was born in Dublin and spent many years abroad, he will be forever associated with the northwestern county of Sligo and the tiny island of Innisfree which he immortalized in his memorable lyric, *The Lake Isle of Innisfree.* In Sligo Town and the lovely rolling green country around it there are not only numerous reminders of his presence but also that of his brother, Jack Butler Yeats, a renowned painter. These buns or cakes are like those I enjoyed there.

2 cups all-purpose flour
2 tablespoons sugar
4 teaspoons baking powder
½ teaspoon salt
⅓ cup cold vegetable shortening
¼ cup light cream or milk
½ cup raisins
Milk and sugar for topping

Preheat oven to 425 degrees.

In a large bowl combine the flour, sugar, baking powder, and salt. With a pastry blender, cut in shortening until mixture is like fine crumbs. Add cream or milk and raisins. Mix quickly to form a soft and sticky dough. Gather into a ball.

Place on a lightly floured surface. With floured hands, knead gently a few turns. Roll or pat into a ½-inch thick circle. With a floured 2-inch cutter, cut into rounds. Transfer to an ungreased baking sheet, placing about 1 inch apart. Prick tops with tines of a fork. Brush tops lightly with milk; sprinkle with sugar.

190

Bake in preheated oven until light golden and puffed, 12 to 15 minutes. Transfer to a wire rack. Cool about 5 minutes. Serve warm with butter and honey or at room temperature with fruit preserves. Makes 24.

# Cakes
# and
# Cookies

*Valentia View. We stopped here for tea and scones.*

193

*In Ireland "There were Cake Dances . . . and an account exists of one in County Mayo near Newport where the cake was placed on a pole and each dancer paid to join the dance. Who-ever paid most and danced most got the cake. An old country superstition is 'to nip the cake,' that is, when a cake is freshly baked a small piece is broken off to avert bad luck. Children sometimes overdo this custom!"*

— *Irish Traditional Food*

"**T**hank God for tea!" wrote the 19th century clergyman and writer Sydney Smith. "What would the world do without tea?" The British passion for tea is a well known phenomenon and it was the English who made the drink famous. But what would the Scots and Irish do without their aromatic, refreshing beverage and all the beloved little delicacies that they enjoy with it? For the Gaels it's always a time for tea: morning, noon and evening.

As a social occasion, afternoon tea has long epitomized charm and taste, imparting a sense of civilized well-being. It also brought out the best of the inherent Gaelic talent for baking. The Scottish and Irish housewife takes great pride in serving her homemade treats including cakes and cookies (called biscuits) for the cherished "meal of ceremony."

Although tea has long played an important role in the daily Gaelic routine, its acceptance was slow, denounced by both the clergy and medical men as sinful and bad for the health. Initially an expensive beverage, prices gradually fell and by the late 18th century tea was no longer a luxury for the gentry. Gradually it became the custom for all classes to enjoy a cup of tea and light refreshments in the home, a ritual for family and friends to this day in Scotland and Ireland.

The habit of going out for tea began, however, in Glasgow where in 1875, Stuart Cranston, a tea dealer, first arranged for customers to buy a cup of the beverage with ". . . bread and cakes extra . . ." But it was his far-seeing talented sister Catherine, or Kate, who, combining business and art, made the tea rooms famous.

Beginning in 1878, when Kate opened her first place in the basement of a temperance hotel, she created a successful empire of tea rooms with high standards of catering and decor where ladies could enjoy what became a popular interlude: afternoon tea. Clustered primarily in Glasgow's business center as "temperance driven alternatives to the city's gin houses," each place was remarkable for its artistic charm, the achievement of Kate's architect partner, Charles Rennie Mackintosh and his avant garde designs.

Fortunately, the renowned Willow Tea Rooms, at 215-17 Sauchiehall Street—opened in 1903, and designed inside and out by Mackintosh—were restored in 1980 and still have his signature high-backed chairs, murals, and stylish features. They are architectural gems where one can enjoy luncheon or afternoon tea.

In Ireland a traditional place for light meals, including a choice of teas, is Bewley's, a chain with several branches that was founded in 1840 by a Quaker named Joshua Bewley. In Dublin the three-story tea room, noted for its high ceilings, stained-glass windows, dark woods, and fine fare, offers, as the saying goes, "a slice of Irish life," as well as a good assortment of typical breads, cakes, pastries, and other appealing treats.

This is a representative collection of cakes and cookies, delightful for afternoon tea or any occasion, which Gaels serve as symbols of hospitality or "welcomes" for friends and neighbors.

# ❁ CAKES

Cake, a baked sweetened dough, often adorned with icing, is truly a creation for celebrations, honoring all happy occasions—birthdays, christenings, festivals, holidays, and, of course, weddings.

In Gaelic lands, however, cakes began as honey-sweetened oat and barley, and later, wheat breads which were originally baked in the ashes of the hearth. Later, fresh and dried fruits, nuts, and spices as well as spirits, were gradually added. Textures were lightened either by adding eggs or leavening agents and with the addition of fat, especially butter. The baking of cakes was aided by better and more reliable stoves and ovens during the 18th century. Thus the contemporary repertoire includes those of all kinds, differing considerably from the simple creations.

Many of the traditional cakes had a symbolic or religious significance and all rites of passage were marked by special kinds. In Scotland a bride's cake was one to dream on for the selection of a mate. After a wedding meal the bride's mother broke a type of shortbread over the head of her daughter. If it broke into small pieces the meaning was a fruitful marriage; if it remained in large lumps, this boded ill. Funeral cakes were taken to the deceased's home as tributes or gifts. And Halloween cakes included charms that foretold fortunes: a horseshoe for good luck, a coin for wealth, and a ring for marriage.

# ❀ APPLE AND OAT CAKE

Apple cakes are particularly Gaelic, the traditional dessert for a family meal. A good many of the old-time recipes made especially in the autumn included such typical ingredients as oats, honey or sugar, spices and raisins. This is one of the best.

1½ pounds (4 medium) tart cooking apples, such as
    Granny Smith
5 tablespoons brown sugar
¾ teaspoon ground cinnamon
½ cup raisins
½ cup (1 stick) unsalted butter, cold and cut up
1 tablespoon honey
3 cups old-fashioned rolled oats
1 tablespoon grated lemon rind
2 large eggs, beaten
Light or heavy cream

Preheat oven to 375 degrees. Lightly butter and flour a 9-inch round springform pan.

Peel, core and cut apples into 1-inch pieces. In a medium heavy saucepan combine the apples, 4 tablespoons sugar, and cinnamon. Cook, covered, over medium-low heat until apples are soft, about 15 minutes. Remove from heat; add raisins; cool.

Meanwhile, in a small saucepan melt the butter and honey with remaining 1 tablespoon sugar. Turn into a large bowl. Add oats, lemon rind, and beaten eggs; mix well. Spoon one third of oat-egg mixture into prepared pan. Top with half the apple mixture. Repeat the layers, topping with oat-egg mixture.

Bake in preheated oven until the top is golden and the cake is cooked, about 30 minutes. Serve warm, cut into wedges, with cream. 6 servings. (Prepare beforehand and reheat, if desired)

# ❀ IRISH CREAM POUND CAKE

This basic pound cake is flavored with Irish cream liqueur. But vanilla extract can be used as a substitute, if desired.

1 cup (2 sticks) unsalted butter, softened
1 teaspoon Irish cream liqueur
½ teaspoon freshly grated nutmeg
½ teaspoon salt
1 ⅔ cups sugar
5 large eggs
1¾ cups sifted all-purpose flour
Confectioners' sugar

Lightly butter and flour the bottom and sides of a 9 × 5 × 3-inch loaf pan.

In a large bowl combine the butter, Irish liqueur, nutmeg, and salt. Cream until light and fluffy. Gradually add sugar, beating as adding, until well mixed. Add 4 eggs, one at a time, beating after each addition. Gradually stir in flour and then the remaining egg. Beat until smooth. Turn into prepared pan. Place in a cold oven. Turn temperature to 300 degrees. Bake until tester inserted into center comes out clean, 1 hour and 20 minutes. Cool in pan 20 minutes. Remove from pan to a wire rack. Cool. Dust top with confectioners' sugar. Wrap in foil. Store in a cool, dry place 1 to 2 days. Serve the cake cut in thin slices. Makes 1 loaf. 12 to 14 servings.

# ❀ SEEDY CAKE

A delicate fruitcake called seedy or seed cake, flavored with spicy, pungent caraway seeds, has long been a favorite Gaelic afternoon tea specialty, often enjoyed with a glass of Port. Made in several varieties, the old-fashioned tea bread called for several flavorings such as rosewater, brandy and spices. This one, similar to a pound cake, is easy to make and fun to serve. ½ cup (1 stick) unsalted butter, softened

½ cup sugar
3 large eggs
2 cups all-purpose flour
2 teaspoons baking powder
⅛ teaspoon freshly grated nutmeg
½ teaspoon salt
1 tablespoon caraway seeds
⅓ to ½ cup milk

Preheat oven to 350 degrees. Lightly butter and flour the bottom and sides of a 9 × 5 × 3-inch loaf pan.

In a large bowl cream the butter and sugar until light and fluffy. Add the eggs, one at a time, beating to blend well.

Into a medium bowl sift the flour, baking powder, nutmeg, and salt. Stir in caraway seeds. Add to butter-sugar mixture, alternately with milk, using enough to make a smooth firm batter. Turn into prepared pan, spreading evenly. Bake in preheated oven until top is golden and tester inserted into center comes out clean, about 50 minutes. Cool in pan 10 minutes. Remove from pan to a wire rack. Cool. Wrap in foil. Store in a cool, dry place for 1 to 2 days. Serve the cake cut in thin slices. Makes 1 loaf. 12 to 14 servings.

# ❀ IRISH TEA BRACK

This traditional tea cake or bread, like a fruit cake but without butter, is flavored with dried fruits soaked in black tea, and sometimes also Irish whiskey. The word *brack* comes from the Gaelic *brec* which means speckled, i.e. with fruit.

2 bags black tea such as Twinings Irish Breakfast tea
1 cup boiling water
1½ cups golden raisins
1½ cups dried black currants
1 cup light brown sugar
1 tablespoon fresh lemon juice
2 teaspoons grated lemon rind

Place tea bags in a large mixing bowl. Add boiling water. Let steep 5 minutes. Remove tea bags. Add raisins, currants, sugar, lemon juice and rind. Cover with plastic wrap to completely enclose the ingredients. Leave overnight at room temperature.

Preheat oven to 325 degrees. Lightly butter and flour the bottom and sides of a 9 × 5 × 3-inch loaf pan.

2 cups all-purpose flour
2 teaspoons baking powder
½ teaspoon ground cinnamon
½ teaspoon ground allspice
⅛ teaspoon ground cloves
½ teaspoon salt
1 large egg

Into a large bowl sift together the flour, baking powder, cinnamon, allspice, cloves, and salt. Add to tea-fruit mixture. Mix well. Stir in egg; mix again. Turn batter into prepared pan. Bake in preheated oven until top is golden and tester inserted into center comes out clean, 1¼ to 1½ hours. Cool in pan 10 minutes. Remove from pan to a wire rack. Cool. (While still warm brush the top with honey or Irish whiskey, if desired.) Cool. Wrap in foil. Store in a cool, dry place for 1 to 2 days or in an airtight container for several days. Serve the cake cut in thin slices. Spread with butter, if desired. Makes 1 loaf. 12 to 14 servings.

## ❀ GINGERBREAD CAKE

Gaels are very fond of pungent, aromatic ginger which they have long used as a flavoring for several varieties of thin hard breads or cookies, traditionally cut in various shapes, and cakes. Long ago they became associated with holiday celebrations and were often presented as gifts. Now they are served with tea or as desserts. This is a moist, dark cake with an appealing spicy flavor.

½ cup (1 stick) unsalted butter, softened
¾ cup light brown sugar
1 large egg, beaten
2½ cups all-purpose flour
1 teaspoon baking soda
2 teaspoons ground cinnamon
2 teaspoons ground ginger
½ teaspoon ground cloves
¼ teaspoon salt
½ cup dark molasses
½ cup hot water

Preheat oven to 350 degrees. Lightly butter and flour a 9 × 13 × 2-inch rectangular baking pan.

In a large bowl cream the butter and sugar until light and fluffy. Add the egg; mix well. Sift in flour, baking soda, cinnamon, ginger, cloves, and salt, adding alternately with molasses and hot water, mixed together. Beat until smooth and well blended. Turn batter into prepared pan, spreading evenly. Bake in preheated oven until tester inserted into center comes out clean, about 30 minutes. Cool in pan 10 minutes. While still warm, cut into 12 or 14 rectangles. With a spatula remove to a large plate or small plates. Serve warm with whipped cream, if desired, or cold, dusted with confectioners' sugar. 12 or 14 servings.

## ❀ CARROT CAKE WITH CREAM FROSTING

This attractive cake is adorned with an Irish cream-flavored frosting.

2 cups sugar
1½ cups vegetable oil
4 large eggs, beaten
3 cups all-purpose flour
2 teaspoons baking soda
3 teaspoons baking powder
2 teaspoons ground cinnamon
½ teaspoon salt
2 cups finely grated raw carrots
1 cup finely chopped walnuts

Preheat oven to 350 degrees. Lightly butter and flour a 10-inch tube cake pan.
In a large bowl combine the sugar, oil, and eggs. Sift in the flour, baking soda, baking powder, cinnamon, and salt; mix well.

Add carrots and walnuts; mix well. Turn into prepared cake pan, spreading evenly. Bake in preheated oven until tester inserted into center comes out clean, about 50 minutes. Cool in pan 10 minutes. Remove from pan to a wire rack. Cool. Spread with frosting. (Recipe below.) Makes 1 cake. 12 to 14 servings.

FROSTING:
1 cup (2 sticks) unsalted butter, softened
2¼ cups confectioners' sugar
½ teaspoon salt
¼ cup Irish cream liqueur or heavy cream

In a medium bowl cream the butter and sugar until light and fluffy. Add salt and cream; beat again. Spread on cake attractively.

*Pier Tearoom & Shop.*

# ❋ SCOTCH SHORTBREAD

Shortbread, sometimes called Scotch cake, is a unique Scottish creation. While not a bread or a cake, it isn't quite a cookie either. Perhaps it's best described as a rich, slightly sweet cookie-type cake with a pleasing flavor and texture that is crisp and somewhat crumbly.

Though usually associated with Christmas and Hogmanay, New Year's Eve, shortbread makes an enjoyable treat all year round, especially for afternoon tea, and family celebrations. Nothing symbolizes Gaelic hospitality better than a plate of shortbread.

Over the years cooks around the world have created many kinds of shortbread with a diverse number of ingredients. But the traditional rich and "short" one is made with only three primary foods: flour, sugar and butter.

While shortbread is made in various forms, the typical one is finger shaped. Some bakers like to make rounds of dough in cake pans or special circular or wooden stoneware molds bearing traditional Scottish symbols, such as the thistle or heather, which leave a raised pattern on the finished shortbread.

All shortbreads should be pricked over the top with tines of a fork before being baked. This prevents the dough from blistering.

# ❋ TEATIME SHORTBREAD

1 cup (2 sticks) unsalted butter, softened
½ cup sugar
2 cups all-purpose flour
⅛ teaspoon salt

Preheat oven to 325 degrees.

In a large bowl cream the butter and sugar until light and fluffy. Sift in flour and salt. With the fingertips or a wooden spoon rub mixture to gently combine and until dough can be pressed together to form a ball.

Place dough on a lightly floured surface. Roll gently into a large rectangle about ½-inch thick. Mark out finger shapes, 2½ inches long and 1 inch wide. Prick tops of each finger with tines of a fork to form three rows. Cut fingers apart; remove to ungreased baking sheets, placing ½ inch apart.

Put fingers in preheated oven. Reduce heat at once to 275 degrees. Bake until light golden on the bottom, sandy white on top, and firm to the touch, 25 to 30 minutes. Watch the color while baking so the dough does not become brown. With a spatula, remove fingers to wire racks to cool. Wrap in wax paper or foil, or store in airtight containers. Serve sprinkled with granulated or confectioners' sugar, if desired. Makes about 3 dozen.

# ❋ IONA OAT-NUT BARS

Iona, a remote tiny isle, just off the coast of Scotland's Mull, is where St. Columba and twelve companions landed in 563, having made passage in a wicker boat from Ireland, and founded a monastery. For centuries Iona was the burial place of Scottish kings and chiefs. On the site of the monastery stands a cruciform Cathedral, and in front of it is St. Martin's Cross, an elaborately carved monument from Celtic days. During my visit to the famous isle I enjoyed a cup of tea and biscuits or cookies made with oats and golden syrup. These crisp bars with a butter-sugar topping are similar to a kind served there.

½ cup (1 stick) unsalted butter, softened
¼ cup confectioners' sugar
1 cup all-purpose flour
½ cup rolled oats
¾ cup light brown sugar
½ teaspoon baking powder
1 cup finely chopped walnuts
2 large eggs, beaten
1 teaspoon vanilla extract

Preheat oven to 350 degrees. Lightly butter the bottom and sides of a 8- or 9-inch square baking pan.

In a medium bowl cream the butter and sugar until light and fluffy. Add the flour; mix well. Turn into prepared baking pan, spreading evenly. Bake in preheated oven 20 minutes.

Meanwhile, in a medium bowl combine the oats, sugar, baking powder, and walnuts. Stir in eggs; mix well. Add vanilla. Spoon over baked mixture, spreading evenly. Return to oven. Continue baking until tester inserted into center comes out clean and mixture is crisp, 12 to 15 minutes. Cool in pan 10 minutes. With a sharp knife cut into 16 squares. Transfer to a wire rack to cool. Makes 16 squares.

# ❀ ROCK CAKES

Flavored with spices and currants, these small cakes or buns are rocky-looking mounds, great favorites for afternoon tea and in-between meal snacks. They are easy and simple to prepare and keep well.

2 cups all-purpose flour
1½ teaspoons baking powder
½ teaspoon ground cinnamon
¼ teaspoon ground nutmeg
⅛ teaspoon ground cloves
½ teaspoon salt
3 tablespoons light brown sugar
½ cup (1 stick) unsalted butter, cool and diced
½ cup dried black currants or raisins
1 large egg
About ½ cup milk

Preheat oven to 400 degrees. Lightly butter and flour a baking sheet.

Into a large bowl sift the flour, baking powder, cinnamon, nutmeg, cloves, and salt. Mix in the sugar. With a pastry blender, cut in butter until mixture is uniformly crumbly. Stir in currants or raisins. Add egg and enough milk to make a stiff dough. Mound the dough, using about 2 tablespoons for each mound, on prepared baking sheet, about 1 inch apart.

Bake in preheated oven until tester inserted into center of a mound comes out clean, about 15 minutes. Transfer cakes to wire racks. Cool. Sprinkle with sugar on top, if desired. Makes about 3 dozen.

# ✸ CHEWY OATMEAL COOKIES

Every Gael loves oatmeal cookies. These are flavored with honey and cinnamon, and include raisins and walnuts. They're great for parties or picnics.

½ cup (1 stick) unsalted butter, softened
¾ cup honey
1 large egg, beaten
1 cup all-purpose flour
½ teaspoon baking soda
¾ teaspoon ground cinnamon
½ teaspoon salt
3 cups quick-cooking rolled oats
2 tablespoons cold water
½ cup finely chopped walnuts
¾ cup raisins

Preheat oven to 350 degrees. Lightly butter 2 baking sheets.

In a large bowl cream the butter and honey. Add the egg; mix well. Sift in flour, baking soda, cinnamon, and salt. Mix well. Stir in oats, then the water, walnuts, and raisins.

Drop by tablespoons on prepared baking sheets, about 1 inch apart. Flatten slightly. Bake in preheated oven until tester inserted into center comes out clean and golden, 10 to 12 minutes. With a spatula remove to a wire rack. Cool. Store in airtight containers. Makes about 4½ dozen.

# ✿ HOLIDAY SPICE COOKIES

These thin, well-seasoned cookies can be cut into various shapes to suit the occasion, from circles to Santas.

½ cup (1 stick) unsalted butter, softened
½ cup light brown sugar
¼ cup white sugar
1 large egg
Grated rind of ½ lemon
2 teaspoons ground cinnamon
½ teaspoon ground nutmeg
¼ teaspoon ground cloves
Salt
2 cups all-purpose flour
2 tablespoons and about 1 teaspoon milk

Preheat oven to 375 degrees.

In a large bowl cream the butter with the brown and white sugars until light and fluffy. Add the egg; beat again. Stir in grated rind. Mix in the cinnamon, nutmeg, cloves, and salt. Sift in flour, a little at a time, alternating with the milk, adding enough to make a fairly stiff but pliable dough. When well mixed, divide into 2 parts. With a floured rolling pin roll out on a floured board to an ⅛-inch thickness. Cut into small bars or any desired shape.

Place on baking sheets. Bake in preheated oven until golden brown, about 15 minutes. Remove to a wire rack to cool. Makes about 2 dozen, depending on the shapes.

# ❀ ORKNEY BROONIE

This is a traditional oatmeal gingerbread from the Orkney Islands that can be eaten as a cake or cookie. The word is said to have come from the Norse *brun*, meaning brown.

1 cup rolled oats
¾ cup all-purpose flour
¼ cup light brown sugar
½ teaspoon baking soda
1 teaspoon ground ginger
⅛ teaspoon salt
3 tablespoons unsalted butter, cold and diced
2 tablespoons dark molasses
1 large egg, beaten
½ cup buttermilk

Preheat oven to 350 degrees. Lightly flour and butter a 8- or 9-inch square cake pan.

Process oats in a blender or food processor, with metal blade in place, until ground to a fine texture.

In a large bowl combine the oats, flour, sugar, soda, ginger, and salt. With a pastry blender, cut in butter until mixture is uniformly crumbly. Add molasses; mix well.

In a small dish whisk the egg and buttermilk. Add to oat-molasses mixture, mixing well to make a stiff batter. Turn into prepared pan, spreading evenly. Bake in preheated oven until tester inserted into center comes out clean, 30 to 35 minutes. Cool in pan 10 minutes. While still warm, cut into 16 squares. With a spatula remove to a large plate. Serve warm or cool. Makes 16.

# *Desserts*

*The Caledonian Hotel, known for its desserts. Oban.*

213

*"The making of butter is likely to have been introduced into Britain by the Celts during the pre-Roman Iron Age. . . . Celts considered butter their choicest food, 'the one that distinguishes the wealthy from the lower orders,' and . . . they usually made it from cow's milk (hence its name boutyron or cow cheese) . . ."*

*— Food and Drink in Britain*

As a method of keeping butter—a key ingredient in Scottish and Irish desserts—fresh, the Celts buried barrels of it in peatbogs where, in recent years, archaeologists have found quantities of the ancient food hidden along with such treasures as jewelry and golden cups underneath the water-logged ground. Two of the mysteries about the "bog-butter" is how it was edible after being stored in the peat and why it was never collected.

From earliest times, Gaels have treasured butter as a basic food for cooking, to use as a spread on breads, and to make desserts. The Scots and Irish have a passion for toothsome sweets, ranging from blissfully airy creations to sinfully rich puddings and pies and, over the years, they created a notable variety of these treats with a few basic ingredients, especially cream, honey, and fruit, as well as butter.

Our word dessert derives from the French verb *desservir*, meaning "to clear the table." After the practice of dividing a meal's dishes into courses became the norm, it was customary to offer an elaborate presentation of sweets when everything had been removed or "disserved" from the dining table. Now the selection of "afters," as they sometimes are called by the Gaels, is limited to usually one, or perhaps a few specialties. But each will be a superb creation carefully prepared with the very best of foods.

Probably the first Gaelic desserts were hearty puddings made by combining grains, fruits, and nuts, sweetened with honey and wine or liqueurs. Yet, over the years home and professional cooks developed such a diverse variety of baked, boiled or steamed sweet puddings that the name actually meant dessert.

Dating back to Celtic times, honey was the principal sweetening agent. The Celts' practice of taking bees to the heather and other rich flora in the summer produced a large supply of exceptional flavors. Gaels use the treasured sweet as a spread for scones or soda bread, in making breads and desserts, as well as drinks and liqueurs of all sorts.

When sugar was introduced into Scotland and Ireland during the 17$^{th}$ century, it, along with spices, would have a great influence on tastes and cookery. Today, despite the generous consumption of sugar, honey is still used a great deal as a sweetener.

While travelling in Gaelic lands I always am delighted to find that dessert is customarily the highlight of a meal. For no repast is considered worthy of guests without the home's favorite "after." Of particular interest are the fascinating "cold sweets" made with recipes from years gone by when dairy products were esteemed foods, and calories weren't counted. Oats play a key role in many of them.

I also am fond of fruit tarts, berry crumbles, latticed pies, filmy light creams, fanciful meringues, and silken smooth custards that are staples in pubs, restaurants, and family-run guest houses.

Gaelic fruits are especially luscious and the great number of orchards and favorable climatic conditions insure an inviting supply of many kinds eaten fresh, made into creams, pastries and pies, as well as ices. Some of the best desserts, especially those of summer, feature the succulent soft fruits, ripened slowly in mild sunshine, like black and red currants and the highly regarded raspberries, esteemed for a desirable intense flavor.

Fortunately, the love of inviting and exceptional desserts continues in Scotland and Ireland as it has for centuries. Here is a pleasing selection of them to serve on any occasion.

## ❀ AVALON APPLE PIE

Since the days of the Celts, apples have been an important Gaelic food, revered as a divine fruit. In Celtic mythology the Otherworld or Paradise was known as Avalon—Isle of Apples. In Avalon there was no rain, sorrow, or illness and the fruit of life grew abundantly. Today, the rite of bobbing for or catching apples in a tub of water at Halloween dates back to the ancient festival of Samhain. For desserts, Gaels are fond of innovative apple puddings, cakes, and pies such as this one made with applesauce.

2 cups tart applesauce
3 tablespoons unsalted butter, melted
1 cup sugar
½ teaspoon salt
2 tablespoons fresh lemon juice
½ teaspoon grated lemon rind
1 teaspoon ground cinnamon
3 large eggs, slightly beaten
Pastry for 1 9-inch pie shell, unbaked

Preheat oven to 450 degrees.
In a large bowl combine the applesauce, melted butter, sugar, and salt. Mix well. Add lemon juice and rind, cinnamon, and eggs, stirring after each addition. Turn into pastry shell.

Bake in preheated oven 15 minutes. Reduce heat to 325 degrees. Bake until a knife inserted into filling comes out clean, about 1 hour. Cool slightly before serving. 6 to 8 servings.

## ❀ LOCH LOMOND CRANACHAN

A traditional Scottish dessert called cranachan or cream-crowdie was once made with oats, whipped cream, honey, and whisky for Highland harvest celebrations. Now it's an elegant cream sweet prepared in several versions. Many of them include fresh berries, especially blueberries, blackberries or raspberries.

I recall the light, elegant pudding as it was served at a village inn on the western shore of Loch Lomond, the largest, most beautiful, and best known of Scottish lochs, famed for its beloved "yon bonnie banks, . . . and yon bonnie braes" song. On the loch's eastern side is Ben Lomond, rising to a height of 3,194 feet, which offers exhilarating walking and spectacular scenery.

¾ cup old-fashioned rolled oats
1½ cups heavy cream, chilled
3 to 4 tablespoons sugar
3 tablespoons Scotch whisky or Drambuie
3 cups fresh berries, washed and hulled

Toast oats in a small dry skillet over medium heat, stirring frequently, until lightly browned, about 3 minutes. Set aside.

In a chilled large bowl, whip cream until soft peaks form. Gradually add sugar and whisky or Drambuie. Whip until mixture thickens. Fold in toasted oats.

In tall stemmed glasses or a glass serving bowl, layer cream mixture and berries, beginning with a layer of cream and topping with a layer of berries. Serve at once or refrigerate, covered with plastic wrap, up to 4 hours.


## ❀ BUNRATTY CASTLE APPLE CRUMBLE

Bunratty Castle, across the Shannon River at Limerick, and standing on what was a former island, is a storybook battlement complete with towers and turrets, dungeons and drawbridge, that's a popular Irish tourist attraction. There are tales aplenty of dark deeds done here dating back to the 13th century. The castle, built in the early 1400s by the McNamara family, was for a long period an O'Brien stronghold. And at one time the defense of the castle was in the hands of Admiral Penn, the father of William Penn who founded Pennsylvania. After years of neglect the fortress was restored to recreate a 15th century atmosphere.

On the grounds surrounding the castle, a Folk Park has examples of farmhouses and one can see butter-making in a "dash" churn and soda-bread baking in a pot oven over an open fire.

Now Bunratty is alive at night when the castle hosts its celebrated Medieval Banquets in the Great Hall replete with a welcoming glass of mead, a honey-based fermented drink, spirited *ceili* entertainment, and a hearty Irish meal with a traditional dessert.

A crumble is like a homey deep-dish fruit pie in which sweetened apples, berries or other fruit are covered with a crisp oat topping. A sort of cobbler or crisp, it's always a winner.

5 large tart cooking apples, peeled, cored and sliced
1 tablespoon fresh lemon juice
¼ cup sugar
½ teaspoon ground cinnamon

TOPPING:
¾ cup all-purpose flour
¾ cup old-fashioned rolled oats
½ cup light brown sugar
½ teaspoon ground ginger
½ cup (1 stick) unsalted butter, cold and cut up

Preheat oven to 375 degrees. Butter the bottom and sides of a 8- or 9-inch square baking dish.

In the prepared baking dish place sliced apples. Sprinkle with the lemon juice, sugar, and cinnamon.

For the topping, in a medium bowl combine the flour, oats, sugar, and ginger. With a pastry blender, cut in butter until mixture is uniformly crumbly. Spread evenly over the apples to make a topping. Bake in preheated oven until top is golden and crisp, 40 to 45 minutes. Serve warm with Irish Whiskey Cream (recipe below) or cold with vanilla ice cream. 6 servings.

## ❀ IRISH WHISKEY CREAM

2 cups chilled heavy cream
2 tablespoons honey
2 tablespoons Irish whiskey

In a chilled large bowl whip the cream until stiff. Fold in the honey and whiskey. Serve over or with the crumble.

*The Harbor Inn — Bowmore, Islay.*

# ❀ HIGHLAND ATHOLL BROSE

This traditional honey and whisky-flavored cream is a modern dessert that has the same name as an ancient Highland drink enjoyed for many Scottish celebrations, especially Hogmanay, New Year's Eve.

12 tablespoons rolled oats
½ cup Scotch whisky
½ cup honey, preferably heather
2 cups heavy cream, chilled
2 tablespoons confectioners' sugar
⅛ teaspoon freshly grated nutmeg
1½ cups fresh ripe raspberries, washed and drained
Additional 18 fresh raspberries for garnish

Toast oats in a small dry skillet over medium heat, stirring frequently, until lightly browned, about 3 minutes. Set aside.

In a small dish combine the whisky and honey. Leave at room temperature up to 1 hour.

In a chilled large bowl whip the cream until soft peaks form; gradually add whisky mixture, the sugar and nutmeg. Whip until the mixture thickens.

In a glass bowl or 6 stemmed dessert glasses, layer the raspberries, toasted oats, and whipped cream mixture. Garnish the top or tops with raspberries. Refrigerate up to 2 hours before serving. 6 servings.

# ❀ POACHED PEARS

The pear, a close relative of the apple and treasured Gaelic fruit, may be cored and filled with a nut-flavored cream cheese mixture or poached in syrup and served with a flavorful sauce.

12 firm slightly underripe pears
Juice of 2 lemons
2 cups sugar
3 cups water
2 teaspoons vanilla extract
2 10- or 12-ounce packages frozen raspberries, partially thawed
2 tablespoons Drambuie or Irish Cream
Whipped cream

Peel and halve the pears. Scoop out cores and cut out stems. Rub with a little lemon juice to prevent darkening.

In a medium saucepan combine the sugar, water, remaining lemon juice, and vanilla extract. Bring to a boil over high heat. Cook briskly 5 minutes. Add pears and reduce the heat to low. Simmer, covered, until pears are tender, about 10 minutes. Remove pears to a serving dish. Reduce syrup over high heat until thick. Pour over pears. Cool at room temperature. Refrigerate, covered with plastic wrap, until ready to serve.

Meanwhile, purée raspberries in a blender or food processor, with metal blade in place. Turn into a medium bowl. Add Drambuie or Irish Cream.

To serve, spoon chilled pears into a large bowl or individual plates. Top with the berry sauce and whipped cream. 12 servings.

# ❋ DRAMBUIE BLANC MANGE

This French-inspired silken milk pudding called *blanc mange* (white food) is one of the many light Gaelic desserts that are flavored with liqueurs. Drambuie, Scotland's oldest and most famous liqueur, made from Highland malt whisky, heather honey and aromatic herbs, has a romantic history. Legend says the original formula was given by "Bonnie Prince Charlie" to the Mackinnon family of Skye as a thank-you gift for giving him shelter. The name is a contraction of the Gaelic phrase "An dram Buidheach," meaning the drink that satisfies.

3 cups milk
½ cup sugar
5 tablespoons cornstarch
¼ teaspoon salt
2 teaspoons Drambuie
1½ cups raspberries or blueberries

In the top of a double boiler over simmering water, scald 2½ cups milk. Meanwhile, in a medium bowl combine remaining ½ cup of cold milk, sugar, cornstarch, and salt. Add ¼ cup of hot milk; mix well. Add to hot milk in top of double boiler. Cook slowly, stirring occasionally, until thickened and smooth, about 15 minutes. Remove from heat; cool. Stir in Drambuie. Turn into a shallow serving bowl. Refrigerate, covered, 4 hours, up to 8 hours. Serve topped with berries. 4 servings.

# ❀ IRISH LEMON PUDDING

A light pudding made from flour, eggs, sugar, milk, and a flavoring is called a sponge. When baked, the bottom creamy custard is spooned over the cake-like topping. This lemony version is a traditional family dessert in Ireland and Scotland.

¼ cup (½ stick) unsalted butter, softened
¾ cup sugar
3 large eggs, separated
⅓ cup fresh lemon juice
1 tablespoon grated lemon rind
⅓ cup all-purpose flour
About ¼ teaspoon salt
1½ cups light cream or milk
Pinch cream of tartar
Confectioners' sugar

Preheat oven to 350 degrees. Butter the sides and bottom of a 1½-quart round baking dish.

In a large bowl cream the butter and sugar until light and fluffy. Mix in egg yolks, one at a time, beating after each addition, and the lemon juice and rind, flour, and ¼ teaspoon salt. Stir to blend ingredients. Gradually add cream or milk, beating as adding. Mix again.

In a medium bowl beat egg whites with a pinch of salt and cream of tartar. Fold gently into batter. Turn into prepared dish. Set dish in a deep ovenproof pan. Add boiling water to reach halfway up the sides of dish.

Bake in preheated oven until puffed and top is golden, about 50 minutes. Remove from oven. Sprinkle with confectioners' sugar. To serve warm, spoon top mixture onto small plates; cover with sauce. 4 to 6 servings.

# ❀ BLACKBERRY FOOL

A delightful and refreshing dessert made simply with a subtle combination of puréed sweetened fruit folded into whipped cream, and usually a flavoring, is called a fool. The origin of the amusing name is not certain but it probably comes from the French *fouler*, meaning to crush. At one time it was synonymous with the word trifle that meant something of little consequence or a bit of foolishness.

Gaels are fond of fools made with sharply flavored fruit like pale green gooseberries, rhubarb, black currants, or citrus fruit juice as well as blackberries or raspberries.

3 cups fresh blackberries
½ cup sugar, preferably superfine
3 tablespoons Drambuie or Irish cream
1½ cups heavy cream, chilled
Whole blackberries for garnish

In a blender or food processor, with metal blade in place, purée blackberries with ¼ cup sugar. Turn into a large bowl. Add Drambuie or Irish cream.

In a chilled large bowl whip the cream until soft peaks form. Gradually add remaining ¼ cup sugar. Whip until mixture thickens. Fold in blackberry purée. Spoon into a large glass bowl or 6 stemmed dessert glasses, dividing evenly. Garnish tops with 1 or 2 whole blackberries. Refrigerate, covered with plastic wrap, up to 4 hours. 6 servings.

# ❀ WHIPT SYLLABUB

A syllabub or sillyboo, is, like a fool, a delightful cream pudding but it has a powerful alcoholic content. The name is believed to derive from a wine that once came from Sillery in France's Champagne region. Bub was slang for a bubbling drink. Traditional recipes called for a pleasing combination of wine, perhaps brandy, sometimes fruit juice, and always sugar. Other liquors or cider as well as spices were added to some variations. This version calls for cider and Irish whiskey.

½ cup sweet or hard cider
2 tablespoons Irish whiskey
½ cup sugar, preferably superfine
⅛ teaspoon freshly grated nutmeg
2 cups heavy cream, chilled
Chocolate shavings for garnish

In a small bowl combine the cider, whiskey, ¼ cup sugar, and nutmeg. Mix well. Leave at room temperature up to 1 hour.

In a large chilled bowl whip the cream until soft peaks form. Gradually add the remaining ¼ cup sugar; whip until stiff. Fold in cider-whiskey mixture. Spoon into a glass bowl or serving dish. Refrigerate, covered with plastic wrap, 2 hours, up to 8 hours, to blend flavors. Serve garnished with chocolate shavings. 6 servings.

# ❀ BAKED APPLES

One can always rely on a warm baked apple for a pleasurable dessert. These are filled with a liqueur-flavored honey-walnut mixture.

½ cup honey
½ cup finely chopped walnuts
1 tablespoon fresh lemon juice
2 tablespoons Drambuie, Irish cream or apple juice
¼ teaspoon freshly grated nutmeg
6 large baking apples (Rome Beauty, York, Jonathan, Cortland)
6 teaspoons unsalted butter, softened

Preheat oven to 350 degrees.

In a small dish combine the honey, walnuts, lemon juice, Drambuie, Irish cream or apple juice, and nutmeg.

Using an apple corer, core the apples from the stem end without cutting through to the bottom. Peel the skin of each apple ⅓ of the way down from the stem end. Arrange apples in a shallow baking dish. Fill the cavities with the honey-nut mixture, sealing each one with 1 teaspoon butter. Pour enough warm water into the dish to cover the bottom of it. Bake, covered, in preheated oven until apples, when pierced with a skewer are tender, about 40 minutes. With a large spoon, remove to a serving dish or individual small plates. Serve warm or at room temperature, topped with a dollop of whipped cream or a spoonful of vanilla ice cream, if desired. 6 servings.

# ❀ TRIFLE

Trifle, a layered arrangement of cake or cookies, custard, fruit and whipped cream, generally flavored with wine or liquor, is an old Christmas and New Year's specialty served attractively in a handsome glass bowl. Because of its alcohol content the cold pudding is also called Tipsy Laird (Lord) by the Scots and Tipsy Cake by the Irish. This is one of many versions.

4 large egg yolks
⅓ cup sugar
⅛ teaspoon salt
1½ cups milk, scalded
½ teaspoon almond extract
10 ladyfingers, split lengthwise
½ cup strawberry or raspberry jam
1 cup finely crumbled macaroons
½ cup sherry, Drambuie or Irish cream
½ cup blanched, slivered almonds
1 cup heavy cream, whipped
⅓ cup confectioners' sugar
½ teaspoon vanilla extract
Glacé or candied cherries

In the top of a double boiler whisk egg yolks, sugar and salt. Gradually pour in scalded milk. Place pan over medium-high heat. Cook egg-milk mixture over simmering water, stirring constantly, until mixture thickens and coats the spoon, about 7 minutes. Remove pan from hot water and place in a pan of cold water to cool. Stir in almond extract. Refrigerate, covered with plastic wrap, 1 to 2 hours.

Spread one side of each ladyfinger with jam. Arrange in a large glass dish. Sprinkle with crumbled macaroons. Pour sherry,

Drambuie or Irish cream over ingredients. Let soak for 15 minutes. Top with chilled custard. Sprinkle with almonds. Refrigerate 1 to 2 hours.

In a chilled large bowl, whip the cream until soft peaks form. Gradually add the confectioners' sugar and vanilla. Whip until mixture thickens. Spread over custard in swirls. Garnish the top with cherries. Serve at once. Or refrigerate, covered with plastic wrap, up to 2 hours before serving. 8 servings.

## ❀ HATTIT KIT

Some of the most beloved Gaelic desserts are called milkmeats or creams, made simply with milk or cream, and a sweetener, flavoring, and perhaps a spirit. One of the ancient Highland treasures is Hattit Kit, also known as Hatted or Added Kit, made originally by milking the cow over a bowl of warm buttermilk. The curd forms over the whey to be a "hat." Kit is the name of a special dish in which the cream was made.

This is a modern version of a cream sweet made with yogurt, cream cheese, and flavorings. It's easy to prepare for an impromptu dessert.

1 cup plain yogurt, drained
½ cup softened cream cheese
3 tablespoons confectioners' sugar
1 teaspoon fresh lemon juice
1 tablespoon Drambuie or orange juice
1 tablespoon orange marmalade

In a medium bowl whip the yogurt, cheese, sugar, and lemon juice to blend well. Stir in Drambuie or orange juice. Refrigerate, covered with plastic wrap, 1 hour, up to 8 hours.

Serve in a glass bowl, garnished on the top with orange marmalade. Place in center of a large plate and surround with oatcakes, shortbread, or tea bread slices. Makes 1½ cups.

## ❀ LEMON CURD

A time-honored British preserve, called lemon curd, cheese, or butter, is a delicately tart and tangy treat that has many roles. It's great as a spread on toast, scones or oatcakes, and can be used to fill pastries. Or, use as a dip for hulled whole strawberries.

2 large eggs
2 egg yolks
½ cup sugar
½ cup fresh lemon juice (2 to 3 lemons)
2 teaspoons grated lemon rind
6 tablespoons butter, cold and cut up

In a heavy medium saucepan whisk eggs, egg yolks, and sugar to blend. Stir in lemon juice and rind, and butter. Place pan over medium-low heat and cook egg-lemon mixture, whisking constantly, until butter melts and sauce thickens, about 5 minutes. Do not boil or overcook or mixture will curdle. Remove from heat. Pour at once into a clean jar or container. Cover; cool; refrigerate. The curd will keep refrigerated up to 2 weeks. Makes 1½ cups.

# ✽ A CHEESE BOARD

The tradition of cheesemaking in Scotland and Ireland goes back to the Celts. Fortunately, the old formulas and skills of the farmhouse have been passed down through the generations and adapted by modern small companies and individuals to make a superb selection of contemporary cheeses. Now dozens of handmade cheeses are on the market. While a number of them are unique to and sold in regions where they are made, more of them are becoming increasingly available in other areas. There also is, of course, a notable variety of cheeses from industrial creameries.

An attractive cheese board of cheeses and appropriate accompaniments is standard fare at pub parties and buffets and makes an excellent dessert. For it, arrange three, four, or more assorted hard and soft cheeses on a breadboard or wood cheese board. Texture and flavor contrasts are desirable when considering choices. All cheeses are better served at room temperature. Remove from refrigerator 1 to 2 hours before serving so that flavors will be at their best. Cover lightly with foil or wax paper until ready to serve.

For accompaniments, offer lightly seasoned or plain crackers, oatcakes, or breads—firm textured white or rye rounds or squares, oat and barley rolls or slices, plain scones or soda breads, or crusty French bread.

One of the easiest and best ways to end a meal is to serve cheese with a complementary fruit, especially those that can be eaten with the fingers: grapes, crisp apple or pear slices, black cherries, or strawberries.

Although nearly any kind of cheese tastes good with apples, a universal favorite is Cheddar, ranging from mild to sharp in taste and from white to deep orange in color. It should be firm and dry with an almost crumbly texture. Both Scotland and

Ireland make excellent regional Cheddar cheeses, mild or mature. These include Scottish Arran, Campbeltown, Islay, Kirkwall, Orkney, and Rothesay as well as Dunlop from Arran and Islay, similar to Cheddar but with a more mellow flavor and softer creamier texture; and the Kerrygold Vintage Irish Cheddar and Ballycashel Cheddar.

Another good combination is a variety of pears, including Anjou, Barlett, Bosc or Comice, and a blue cheese such as Stilton, Scottish Stewart, Arran or Brodick Blue and Irish Cashell Blue.

# Drinks

*I walked past this tavern on my way to the harbor—*
*Scottish coast.*

235

> "From the Brehon law tracts it may be gathered that the priv-
> ileges of an Irish king included the right to have his ale sup-
> plied him with food; he was also to have a brave army and an
> inebriating ale-house. The Irish chief is always to have two
> casks in his house, one of ale, another of milk. . . ."
> — *the curiosities of ALE & BEER*

The captivating drinks of Scotland and Ireland are known around the world as esteemed libations. In Gaelic lands drinking strong spirits has long been an important element of everyday living and all celebrations.

Where to begin? Near the beginning, maybe, with a liquor called mead, made from fermented honey and water, usually flavored with herbs. Said to have been brewed very far back in history, mead was the warrior's drink, as well as that of the upper-class Celts, and was consumed in great quantities at royal banquets, especially those held at Tara, seat of Ireland's High Kings.

Through the years mead, believed to have powers of virility and fertility, became associated with weddings. The word honeymoon is said to have come from the tradition of toasting the bride and groom with goblets of mead and giving them enough of the drink with appropriate glasses to last for one full moon after the wedding.

Today, mead is once again being made with an ancient formula and enjoyed as an aperitif or "wine." It is also served at Ireland's popular medieval castle banquets and used as an ingredient in cooking, especially meat and poultry dishes. The Bunratty Winery, an old coach house situated in the shadow of the now famous Bunratty Castle, produces the mead served there. Their mead is sold not only in Ireland but also in some U.S.A. locales (as meade).

# ❊ ALE

Dating back to the days of the ancient Celts, beer brewed from malted barley has been a favorite drink in Scotland and Ireland. But the most traditional brew is an ale. Made from malt and hops and produced by rapid fermentation at a relatively high temperature, the treasured drink comes in a broad spectrum of flavors, colors, and strengths.

The earliest known is heather ale which predates history, brewed in Scotland since 2000 B.C. According to legend, Pictish kings preferred to die rather than reveal the formula for making the drink, and Celtic sorcerers gave it to their warriors before battle. The residents of the mythical Scottish community of Brigadoon are said to have brewed their own ale. And, in the words of Robert Louis Stevenson, it "Was sweeter far than honey, Was stronger far than wine."

More than 250 years after being outlawed by the King of England, the legendary drink is again brewed in Scotland under the name Fraoch Heather Ale. Available on draught in Scotland throughout the heather flowering season of July to October, the classic ale is also sold in bottles in many countries, including the United States.

What the Scots and Irish call "real ales" are naturally conditioned cask ales, served in pubs hand-pulled from pumps. They taste fresher, are richer and usually darker than fizzy "keg" ales that are generally heat pasteurized and filtered. A good ale should be served cool—not cold or iced.

Scotland has a distinct brewing tradition and is noted for its malty ales. Favorite brands are creamy, dark brown McEwan's Scotch Ale; Belhaven, a classic; the very strong MacAndrew's; and earthy Traquair House Ale.

Ireland makes good lager, notably the dry pale full-bodied Harp, and is known for its Smithwick's Ale that comes from the St. Francis Abbey in Kilkenny.

# ✸ STOUT

In 1759, when Arthur Guinness came to Dublin to try his luck
at business by leasing a small, disused brewery at St. James's
Gate, he began by making ale and then a dark drink known as
porter. Popular in the 18th and 19th centuries, its name is said to
have originated from the porters of London's Covent Garden who
drank a lot of it.

Like other substantial brews it became known as stout
porter, and then simply stout, meaning "hearty" and "robust," a
drink that is a stronger, fuller-bodied creamier style of porter. It's
a specific kind of beer that is somewhat bitter in taste with a
strong malt flavor and characteristic dark brown color that comes
from the roasted barley.

Stout is made in several countries but notably Ireland where
Guinness established not only a successful business but a tradition exceptional in brewing history. For his "new" superior stout
quickly became the Irish national drink, poured from draft taps
and downed in pints, topped with a dense, creamy white head, in
every convivial pub. Today, the "robust, mellow and satisfying"
Extra Stout Guinness is also sold in recognizable brown bottles
around the world, associated with Irishness everywhere. The
beloved tipple was aptly dubbed by James Joyce as "the wine
of Ireland."

Made from hops, roasted barley, yeast, and pure Dublin
water, Guinness has long been touted by the Irish as a healthy
drink. For it was brilliantly marketed with the slogan "Guinness
is Good for You," and a picture of the Guinness drinker cap-
tioned, "Health, Peace and Prosperity." The brew also was her-
alded as a medicinal miracle, used for everything from a tonic to
a pain killer.

Stout has a natural affinity for food and goes extremely well
with shellfish, especially oysters, cheeses and cheese dishes, as

well as all kinds of picnic and pub fare. It imparts a fine flavor to soups and stews, and, along with moistness, to the texture of breads and holiday fruit cakes and puddings.

Stout is also a popular ingredient in drinks: mixed with champagne to make the elegant Black Velvet, and with lager for a libation called Black and Tan in the United States and Half and Half in Ireland.

The present Guinness Brewery covers a vast complex along Dublin's Liffey River, and is one of the city's historic sites. At the "World of Guinness" exhibition housed in the Guinness Hop Store on Crane Street, visitors can learn a lot about the history of brewing, everything from the firm's transport to advertising posters. They can also enjoy a glass of the national brew in a traditional pub setting.

Two other Irish stouts, Murphy's, a softer, more delicate brew than Guinness, and Beamish, dry and silky, are made in County Cork.

## ❀ WHISKY/WHISKEY

Although the Irish claim to have invented whisky or whiskey and that the technique of distilling it from grain was brought to Scotland from Ireland, there is some evidence that it spread eastwards from the west coast. Suffice it to say that the facts about the origins of the drink are not known. But the history of the libation is closely linked to that of each country.

The earliest documentary reference to whisky appears in the Scottish Exchequer Rolls of 1494—"eight bolls of malt to Friar John Cor . . . to make *aqua vitae*." The name whisky derives from the Gaelic *uisce-beatha*, meaning the water of life.

By the 15<sup>th</sup> century the technique of distilling malt to make a fierce, smoky brew was well established in the Highlands. Much of the whisky was distilled illegally, and men fought battles over the right to make the drink.

The world-famous Scotch whisky, always spelled without the "e," is a unique creation because it cannot be produced elsewhere. The secret of its special character involves the Scottish pure clear water, superb barley and peat, and even the climate.

Blending of the strong Highland whisky with a milder Lowland whisky began in the 1860s. Today most Scotch whisky is a blend of the flavorful malt with a lighter cereal spirit. Pure whiskies from Scotland's individual distilleries are known as single, or unblended, malts. Long considered the aristocrats of Scotch, they are full-flavored, smooth and assertive—like the Scots, some say.

All single malts are best drunk neat, without ice, or as they do in Scotland, with a splash of cool spring water to bring out the aroma.

"These generous whiskies, with their individual flavors, recall the world of hills and glens, of raging elements, of shelter, of divine ease," wrote Neil Gunn.

Ah, but in Ireland the classic drink is whiskey, spelled with an "e," which has a long and notable history. For centuries, home-distilled *uisce beatha* was a highly prized drink, enjoyed by royalty and explorers, including Sir Walter Raleigh. In his famed Dictionary, Dr. Samuel Johnson praised the Irish libation as "particularly distinguished for its pleasant and mild flavour."

Earlier, in the mid-1500s, another Englishman, Richard Stanihurst, sang its praises with these words:

"... it sloweth age; it strengtheneth youth; it helpeth digestion; it cutteth fleume; it abandoneth melancholie; it relisheth the harte; it lighteneth the mynd; it quickeneth the spirites; it cureth the hydropsie; ... trulie a soverign liquor. ..."

By the 17<sup>th</sup> century distilling was flourishing in Ireland and Bushmills, the oldest licensed whiskey distillery in the world, located in the village of Bushmills, County Antrim, Northern Ireland, was founded in 1603. Interestingly, this was along the River Bush on an old road between Tara, Ireland's ancient capital, and Dunseverick Castle where St. Patrick is said to have visited.

Today visitors to Bushmills may take entertaining and informative tours of the distillery where the smooth, light Old Bushmills Irish Whiskey, is still produced, and enjoy a drink in the Postill Bar. An exhibition area has been created in what were once old malt kilns.

Like Scotch whisky, Irish whiskey is pot-still produced but it is triple-distilled instead of the usual two as in Scotland. Another important difference in the distilling is that the malt is not exposed to peat smoke. Thus the drink has a distinct smooth, mellow and smokeless taste. Some devotees refer to it as warm-hearted or comforting. It is best drunk neat or with a little cold water. Hot, it's good flavored with sugar, lemon and cloves. Although the whiskey is used to make a few drinks, notably Irish coffee, it is not a good mixer.

While Ireland's best known whiskey brands include Bushmills, John Jameson, John Power, Paddy, and smooth, rich Tullamore Dew, there are several excellent more recent drinks such as Kilbeggan.

# ❁ LIQUEURS

Other great Scottish and Irish contributions to conviviality are a variety of sweet and colorful liqueurs with highly concentrated flavors, based on the local spirits, sweetened and flavored with aromatic substances. Delicious either on its own, mixed in cocktails or other drinks, a liqueur gives superb flavor to food, savory as well as sweet.

As previously mentioned, delightful Drambuie, Scotland's oldest and most famous liqueur, is made from Highland malt whisky, heather honey and aromatic herbs. It has an attractive sherry-brown color showing flecks of gold in the sun that has been described as "sunbeams imprisoned on a peat bog."

Drambuie has an intriguing history which dates back to the personal life and times of Bonnie Prince Charlie, the Young Pretender to the English throne. Thus the drink is sold around the world as "Prince Charles Edward's Liqueur, A Link With the '45."

The liqueur blends perfectly with Scotch whisky in a number of drinks and is a superb flavoring for food. To make Drambuie coffee, substitute Drambuie for the Irish Whiskey in the Irish Coffee recipe.

Other Scottish liqueurs include Glayva, which in Gaelic means "Very Good." Created in 1799, it's a concentrate of Scotch whisky harmoniously flavored with heather honey, anise, and native Scotch herbs. Glen Mist, made with fine, fully matured whisky, is blended with herbs, honey, and spices. Several of the Scotch whisky companies also produce liqueurs marketed under their brand names.

Irish Mist, one of Ireland's notable liqueurs is made from an ancient recipe for heather wine. The contemporary version is based on four different whiskies, flavored with three honeys (heather, fox glove and clover), plus a dozen hand-picked aromatic herbs. While enjoyed as a drink, the liqueur adds an exquisite flavor to many dishes, especially desserts.

Ireland's most famous liqueur, however, is the rich and luscious Baileys Irish Cream, a delightful combination of the country's fresh dairy cream and whiskey, flavored with pure vanilla and cocoa. A modern business phenomenon, it was first marketed in 1974, and is only produced at Nangor House, County Dublin. The name comes from Dublin's trendy pub, The Bailey, once a favorite of James Joyce and now a meeting place for aspiring writers and actors. For those who prefer less fat or calories, there's also Baileys Light.

After the success of Baileys came other Irish creams such as the honey-flavored Carolans, named for a 17th century harpist, and Saint Brendan's Superior Cream that includes aged whiskey.

Irish creams, best drunk chilled or on the rocks, can be mixed with many spirits and are popular flavorings for a number of desserts, especially those made with chocolate and fruits.

# ❀ PUBS

When considering Scotland and Ireland, one must not forget the great and beloved institution, the public house, better known as the pub. As previously mentioned in the introduction, there are pubs galore and enjoying the informal conviviality of them is a good way to meet the Scots and Irish. Inviting gathering places, possessed of atmosphere and good cheer, pubs, renowned for spirits, fine food, and entertainment, cater to everyone's tastes. Most pubs stock a large choice of excellent brews, and the fare is no longer limited to pickled eggs, sausages, and mundane sandwiches.

While the Scots do love to frequent the pub, it's the Irish who truly enjoy their "home away from home," as it's often called. And, certainly the most famous city in the world for pubs is Dublin, reputed to have at least 600 of them.

Many of the pubs have preserved or re-created their original decor with brass lamps, lovely old mirrors, and stained glass. A traditional Irish pub has snugs, small enclosed "rooms" with hatch openings for drinks to be passed in for discreet imbibing.

In Dublin a good place for a pub crawl, or tour of pubs, is the Temple Bar area, a busy revitalized district in the central part of the city between Trinity College and Christchurch Cathedral. For it's a dynamic mix of pubs, nightclubs, restaurants, art galleries, and hotels.

Some of Dublin's better known pubs are: Abbey Tavern, at Howth, nestled against the ancient ruins of St. Mary's Abbey, featuring lively entertainment with singers and musicians; Brazen Head, reputed to be the city's oldest pub; Davy Byrne's, where Leopold Bloom in Ulysses stopped for a gorgonzola sandwich and a glass of burgundy; The Long Hall, a famous exuberant shrine; Kitty O'Shea's, noted for its great food: McDaid's, a lively place for writers; Mulligan's, noted for its Victorian decor; Neary's, a favorite of Dublin's actors and actresses; O'Donoghue's, a good place to hear traditional Irish music; Toner's, an authentic country pub; and Whelan's, a restored old pub.

*Slainte mhath!* Good Health!

Here are recipes for some traditional and contemporary drinks.

## ❀ ATHOLL BROSE

In Scotland the traditional drink to "warm the festive soul" on Hogmanay, New Year's Eve, is Atholl Brose. Usually an oatmeal, malt whisky, honey, and cream combination, there are many individual and regional variations of the libation, which emerged from the Highland mists in 1475. According to one legend the duke of Atholl, a small town in the Tayside region, poured the drink into the well of his arch enemy, the Earl of Ross, who "drunk deeply of it" and was thus easily captured. This version is made without oatmeal.

1 cup water
1 cup honey, preferably heather
2½ cups Scotch whisky
1 cup light cream

Pour water into a large saucepan. Bring to a boil over medium-high heat. Add honey. Heat, stirring, to dissolve. Gradually add whisky. Stir until mixed well. Add cream. Stir again. Remove from heat. Serve in small or thistle-shaped glasses. Makes about 1¼ quarts.

## ✿ AULD MAN'S MILK

A morning drink or pick-me-up, said to have been the original modern egg nog, is an old Scottish favorite. It can be served in a punch bowl, cup or glass. This is an easy recipe for making an individual cold or hot nog.

1 egg
1 teaspoon sugar
2 to 3 ounces Scotch whisky
8 ounces cold or scalded milk
Freshly grated nutmeg

Combine the egg, sugar, whisky, and milk in a cocktail shaker or large glass. Mix well. Pour into a glass and serve with a dash of nutmeg over the top. Makes 1 drink.

*The Burns Monument Hotel, well-known for serving drinks.*

## ❀ BLACK VELVET

Made from equal parts of chilled champagne and stout, the drink takes its name from the dark color of the stout.

6 ounces (¾ cup) ice cold stout
1 split (about 6 ounces) chilled champagne

Pour stout into a chilled silver mug or tall glass. Carefully pour champagne over it so the two liquors do not mix. Do not stir. Serve at once. Makes 1 drink.

# ❀ CIDER CUP

Cider has a venerable history in Gaelic lands, dating back to the Celts who enjoyed it as an everyday drink, both sweet and hard. It is also a good cooking ingredient, added to pork and fruit dishes as well as desserts.

3 ounces (⅓ cup) cider or applejack
2 tablespoons sugar
2 whole cloves
1 inch cinnamon stick
1 thin slice of lemon

Combine cider or applejack, sugar, cloves, cinnamon stick, and lemon slice in a mug or goblet. Fill with hot water. Stir until sugar is dissolved. Makes 1 drink.


# ❀ GAELIC LEMONADE

4 large lemons
¾ cup hot water
½ cup sugar
6 cups cold water
Gin, Irish whiskey, or Scotch whisky to taste

Roll lemons on a flat surface. Cut in halves; squeeze juice into a pitcher. Slice halves and put in a small bowl. Cover with hot water; cool. Strain and add to lemon juice. Add the sugar and cold water; stir to dissolve sugar; chill in refrigerator. To serve, add gin, whiskey or whisky to taste. Makes 6 drinks.

# ❀ GINGER BEER

A nonalcoholic effervescent beverage flavored with fermented ginger and sold in stoneware bottles was once a popular drink in Scotland. Sometimes called stone ginger beer, the fizzy soft drink was not only enjoyed as a libation but taken as cure for all sorts of illnesses. Now sold in bottles, primarily from Caribbean countries, the beer can be drunk plain or spiked with vodka, rum or whiskey, to make a toddy, if desired.

# ❀ GLASGOW PUNCH

This inviting libation, made with a mixture of sugar, lemon or lime juice, and spirits, was popular in Glasgow clubs or "jovial fraternities" when Caribbean rum was brought by ships to Scotland. Some recipes use brandy instead of the rum.

½ cup sugar, preferably superfine
3½ cups cold water
1 cup lime and lemon juice
¾ cup light rum

Combine sugar and 1 cup cold water in a large pitcher or punch bowl. Stir to dissolve. Add remaining water, lime and lemon juice, and rum. Mix well. Chill in refrigerator until ready to serve. Makes 1¼ quarts.

# ❀ HET PINT

Hot ale, spiced and laced with whisky, was once the great Hogmanay drink. It was carried by lads through town and city streets in copper or toddy kettles shortly before midnight and passed in cupfuls to any passers by. Here's a version of the drink that is great for winter or holiday parties.

2 quarts ale
1 teaspoon freshly grated nutmeg
½ cup sugar
3 large eggs
1 cup Scotch whisky

In a large saucepan combine the ale and nutmeg over medium heat until mixture becomes hot. Do not boil. Add sugar; stir to dissolve. In a medium bowl beat eggs. Add ¾ cup hot ale mixture; beat to blend well. Add to hot ale mixture, stirring while adding. Stir in whisky. Reheat until hot; beat again. Serve at once in mugs. Makes about 2½ quarts.

# ❀ IRISH COFFEE

This famous after-dinner drink, sometimes served as a dessert, is said to have been created by an airline captain at Shannon Airport in the 1950s. According to the legend he prepared the libation, also called Gaelic Coffee, as an eye-opener for travel-weary Americans, including enthusiastic journalists. They brought it to the United States where it became very popular in no time at all.

According to the Irish, the libation should be made with cream rich as an Irish brogue, coffee strong as a friendly hand, sugar sweet as the tongue of a rogue, and whiskey smooth as the wit of the land.

To make, rinse a 6 or 8-ounce stemmed whiskey goblet or Irish coffee glass with hot water. Add 1 teaspoon sugar and enough hot coffee to dissolve sugar. Stir well. Add Irish whiskey to fill within an inch of the brim. Hold a teaspoon curved side up across the glass and pour 1 tablespoon double cream into the coffee. It should float on top. The hot whiskey-laced coffee is drunk through the cold cream. Makes 1 drink.

## ❀ MILK PUNCH

Here's a simple formula for an old favorite.

2 ounces Scotch whisky or Irish whiskey
1 cup cold milk
1 teaspoon superfine sugar
Dash vanilla extract
Freshly grated nutmeg

Combine the whisky or whiskey, milk, sugar, and vanilla with ice in a cocktail shaker. Cover; shake well. Strain into a chilled mug or glass. Sprinkle top with nutmeg. Makes 1 drink.

# ROB ROY

This Scottish drink takes its name from Scotland's outlaw who was depicted in the celebrated movie, *Rob Roy*.

2½ ounces Scotch whisky
½ ounce dry vermouth
2 dashes orange bitters

Pour ingredients into a large mixing glass filled with ice. Stir. Strain into a chilled cocktail glass. Twist a lemon peel over drink, if desired.


## ❋ RUSTY NAIL

1½ ounces Scotch whisky
1½ ounces Drambuie

Pour whisky and Drambuie over ice cubes in a chilled old-fashioned glass. Stir gently. Makes 1 drink.

# ❀ SHANDY

A refreshing long drink made of ale mixed with ginger beer, ginger ale or lemonade, called a shandy or shandy gaff, is a popular pub drink. The origin of the name is unknown. At one time sailors drank the libation as a source of vitamin C.

To make, pour cold ale to half fill a chilled tall glass or mug. Then add cold ginger beer, ale or lemonade to fill the glass. Stir quickly and serve.

# ❀ WHISKY OR WHISKEY TODDY

Mixtures of sweetened spirits and hot water are traditional Gaelic drinks taken to ward off the cold or as a favorite nightcap. One variation called a toddy usually contains a thin slice of lemon.

1 to 2 teaspoons brown or white sugar
3 ounces Scotch whisky or Irish whiskey
2 whole cloves
Dash ground cinnamon
Freshly grated nutmeg
1 thin slice lemon

Heat a stemmed goblet or tall glass by filling with hot water and then throwing it out. Pour in fresh hot water, enough to half fill the glass. Add the sugar. Stir to dissolve. Add the whisky or whiskey, cloves, and cinnamon. Sprinkle with a dash of nutmeg and with lemon slice floating on top. Makes 1 drink.

# BIBLIOGRAPHY

Allen, Darina. *The Festive Food of Ireland*. West Cork: Roberts Rinehart, 1992.

Bickerdyke, John. *the curiosities of Ale & Beer*. London: Spring Books, 1965.

Brown, Catherine. *Scottish Cookery*. Glasgow: Richard Drew, 1997.

Delaney, Frank. *The Celts*. Boston: Little, Brown, 1986.

Delaney, Mary Murray. *Of Irish Ways*. Minneapolis: Dillon, 1973. Fitzgibbon, Theodora.

———*A Taste of Ireland*. New York: Avenel Books, 1971.

———*A Taste of Scotland*. London: Pan Books, 1971.

———*Irish Traditional Food*. London: Pan Books, 1983.

Herm, Gerhard. *The Celts*. New York: St. Martin's, 1975.

Hope, Annette. *A Caledonian Feast*. Edinburgh: Mainstream, 1987.

Johnson, Samuel & James Boswell. *Journey to the Hebrides*. Edinburgh: Canongate Classics, 1996.

Kinchin, Perilla. *Tea and Taste*. Oxford: White Cockade, 1996.

Krasner, Deborah. *From Celtic Hearths*. New York: Viking, 1991.

Livingston, Sheila. *Scottish Customs*. USA: Barnes & Noble, 1996.

McCormick, Malachie. *In Praise of Irish Breakfasts*. Staten Island: The Stone Street Press, 1991.

McKenna, John, and Sally. *The Bridgestone Irish Food Guide*. Cork: Estragon Press, 1993.

McNeill, F. Marian. *The Scots Kitchen*. London: Blackie & Son, 1964.

———*The Scots Cellar*. London: Granada, 1973.

Murphy, Brian. *The World Book of Whiskey*. Chicago: Rand McNally, 1979.

Nelson, Kay Shaw.

——*A Bonnie Scottish Cookbook*. McLean, VA: EPM, 1989.

——*The Best of Western European Cooking*. New York: John Day, 1976.

O'Byrne, Sandy. *The Irish Table*. Dublin: Eason & Son, 1985.

O'Mara, Veronica Jane and Fionnuala O'Reilly. *A Trifle, A Coddle, A Fry*. London: Moyer Bell, 1996.

Shaw, C. *Scottish Myths & Customs*. Glasgow: Harper Collins, 1997.

Sheridan, Monica. *The Art of Irish Cooking*. New York: Doubleday & Co, 1965.

Squire, Charles. *Celtic Myths & Legend Poetry & Romance*. New York: Bell, 1979.

Toulson, Shirley. *Celtic Journeys*. London: Fount Paperback, 1985.

Wagenknecht, Edward. *Sir Walter Scott*. New York: Continium, 1991.

Wilson, C. Anne. *Food and Drink in Britain*. Chicago: Academy, 1991.

# RECIPE INDEX

# SUBJECT INDEX

Fitzgibbon, Theodora, 161
Forfar, Angus, 138
Fraoch Heather Ale, 238
Fuller, Thomas, 31

Gael(s), 1
Gaelic, x, 1–5
Gaeltacht, 87, 137
Gallagher's Boxty House, 187
Galway, 13
  Bay, 13, 86
  City, 13
Giant MacAskill-Highland
      Pioneer's Museum, 70
Gigha, Isle of, 45
Gilmour, Barbara, 38
Glasgow, 195
  Clubs, 249
  Tea Houses, 196
Gregory, Lady, 86
Guaire, King, 86
Guinness
  Arthur, 239
  Brewery, 239, 240
  Stout, 239

Haggis Scotch, 142
Halloween, 3, 130, 187, 197,
      217
Harris, Island of, 178
Hebrides
  Inner, 27
  Outer, 9, 63, 65, 70, 89, 91
Highland(s)
  Games and Gatherings, 138
Hogmanay, 142, 205, 250
Hunt Museum, Limerick, 140

Imbolc, 3, 172
Iona, x, 206
*In Praise of Irish Breakfasts*,
      152
Inverness, 171
Irish
  Achilles, 67
  Counties
    Antrim, 242
    Covan, 187
    Donegal, 137, 187
    Leitrim, 187
Islay, Isle of, 27

Johnson, Dr. Samuel, 50, 108,
      241
*Journey to the Hebrides*, 108
Joyce, James, 130, 239, 244
  *Lives of the Saints*, 159

Keil Point, x
Kerry, Ring of, 121, 145, 184
*Kidnapped*, Robert Louis
      Stevenson, 131
Kilchoman, Isle of Islay, 27
Kildare, 106
  County, 106
  Town, 106
Kildaton, High Cross of, 27
Kilkenny
  Castle, 43
  City, 43
Killagin, Kerry, 121
Killrush, 47
Kintyre Peninsula, ix, x
Kinvara, 86
Kirkwall, Orkney, 73

Orkney
  Isles, 29, 40, 73, 211
  Kirkwall, 73
Oyster Festival, September,
  Galway City, 13

Penn
  Admiral, 219
  William, 219
Picts, x, xi, 238
Posidonius, 123
Potato(es), 147
  Famine, 148
  Irish, 148
  Scottish, 149
*Prelude*, John Synge, 56
Pub(s), 4, 244
  Dublin, 245
  Grub, 4

Raleigh, Sir Walter, 39, 241
Roadside Tavern,
  Lisdoonvarna, 12
Roscommon County, 148
*Roy(s), Rob*, 103
  Folk Hero, 103, 104
  Movie, 103, 252

Saint Ann's, Cape Breton, 70
Salmon of Knowledge, The,
  85
Samhain, 3, 217
Scarp, Island of, 178
Scone(s), 179
Scot(s), xi
Scott, Sir Walter, 84
  *Rob Roy*, 103

*St. Ronan's Wall*, 131
*Scottish Customs*, 49
*Scottish Myths & Customs*,
  65
Seanachie, 25
  Pub, 25
Shamrock, 167
Shand, P. Morton, 31
Shannon
  Airport, 54, 250
  River, 140, 219
Sheridan, Monica, 171
Sillery, 227
Skara Brae, Orkney, 29
Skibbereen, 92
Skye, Isle of, 33, 70, 108,
  224
Sligo
  County, 190
  Town, 190
Smith, Sydney, 195
St.
  Andrew's Night, 142
  Bridget's Day, 3, 106,
    187
  Columba, x, 35, 159, 206
  Finnbarr, 91
  Martin's Cross, 207
  Michael(s)
    Bannock, 174
    Day, 117
  Patrick(s), 32, 167
    Day, 126
  Stephen's Day, 124
Stanihurst, Richard, 241
Stevenson, Robert Louis
  *Kidnapped*, 238

## *Also by Kay Shaw Nelson . . .*

## Cuisines of the Caucasus Mountains
**Recipes, Drinks, and Lore from Armenia, Azerbaijan, Georgia, and Russia**
People of the Caucasus Mountains, a region comprising Armenia, Azerbaijan, Georgia and Russia, are noted for a creative and masterful cuisine that cooks evolved over the years by using fragrant herbs and spices and tart flavors such as lemons and sour plums.

The 184 authentic recipes featured in Cuisines of the Caucasus Mountains offer new ways of cooking with healthful yet delectable ingredients like pomegranates, saffron, rose water, honey, olive oil, yogurt, onions, garlic, fresh and dried fruits, and a variety of nuts. The literary excerpts, legends, and lore sprinkled throughout the book will also enchant the reader-chef on this culinary journey to one of the world's most famous mountain ranges.
288 pages • 6 x 9 • 0-7818-0928-2 • $24.95hc • (37)

## All Along the Rhine
**Recipes, Wines and Lore from Germany, France, Switzerland, Austria, Liechtenstein and Holland**
This wonderful collection of over 130 recipes spans the range of home cooking, from Appetizers, Soups, Main Courses, and Side Dishes, to Desserts and Beverages. Among the recipes included are traditional favorites and signature dishes from the six countries: "Cheese Fondue," "Balzers Split Pea-Sausage Stew," "Alpine Sauerkraut Soup," "Bratwurst in Beer," and "Pears in Red Wine."

Each chapter covers the culinary history and winemaking tradition of a different Rhine country. The literary excerpts, legends and lore throughout the book will enchant the reader-chef on this culinary cruise down one of the world's most famous rivers.
230 pages • 5½ x 8½ • b/w photos • 0-7818-0830-8 • $24.95hc • (89)

## *From Hippocrene's Cookbook Library*

## Feasting Galore, Irish-Style
*Maura Laverty*
Hippocrene Books is pleased to bring this classic cookbook, which was originally published in 1952, back into print for today's readers. Author Maura Laverty, a leading Irish playwright, novelist and culinary writer, beckons readers through the door of the traditional Irish kitchen to the heart of the family's life. Each of the eleven chapters begins with an engaging anecdote that puts the food into its context—whether it is prepared to celebrate an occasion, to welcome guests, or even to seduce! With simple ingredients and easy-to-follow instructions, these 200 recipes will help the home chef create a rich, plentiful Irish feast.
144 pages • 5½ x 8½ • line drawings • 0-7818-0869-3 • $14.95pb • (94)

# Traditional Food from Scotland

A delightful assortment of Scottish recipes and helpful hints for the home—this classic volume offers a window into another era.

336 pages • 5½ x 8 • 0-7818-0514-7 • $11.95pb • (620)

# The Art of Irish Cooking

*Monica Sheridan*

Nearly 200 recipes for traditional Irish fare.

166 pages • 5½ x 8½ • 0-7818-0454-X • W • $12.95pb • (335)

# Celtic Cookbook: Traditional Recipes from the Six Celtic Lands

*Helen Smith-Twiddy*

This collection of over 160 recipes from the Celtic worlds includes traditional, yet still popular dishes like Rabbit Hoggan and Gwydd y Dolig (Stuffed Goose in Red Wine).

200 pages • 5½ x 8½ • 0-7818-0579-1 • NA • $22.50hc • (679)

# *Dictionaries and Language Guides from Hippocrene . . .*

# Hippocrene Children's Illustrated SCOTTISH Dictionary
# English-Scottish/Scottish-English
# &
# Hippocrene Children's Illustrated IRISH Dictionary
# English-Irish/Irish-English

Designed to be a child's very *first* foreign language dictionaries for ages 5 and up, these books includes 500 entries (objects, people, colors, numbers, and activities), each accompanied by a large, full-color illustration. The words are clearly divided into syllables, and a handy pronunciation guide at the beginning of each book allows children and parents to learn the correct way to pronounce each word.

**Scottish dictionary**: 96 pages • 8½ x 11 • 0-7818-0721-2 • W • $14.95 hc • (224)
**Irish dictionary**: 96 pages • 8½ x 11 • 0-7818-0713-1 • W • $14.95 hc • (798)

# Scottish Gaelic-English/English-Scottish Gaelic Dictionary

*R. W. Denton & J.A. MacDonald*

In addition to its 8,500 modern entries, this dictionary features a list of abbreviations, an appendix of irregular verbs, and a grammar guide. The English-Scottish Gaelic section is expanded to facilitate conversations and composition. Geared for both students and travelers, the handy size and thorough vocabulary make it a perfect traveling companion throughout the Scottish highlands.

162 pages • 4 x 6 • 8,500 entries • 0-7818-0316-0 • NA • $8.95pb • (285)

## Ogham: An Irish Alphabet
*Críostóir Mag Fhearaigh*
*Illustrated by Tim Stampton*
This book includes a bilingual explanation and an illustrated representation of the ancient and enigmatic Ogham alphabet.
80 pages • 5½ x 8½ • 0-7818-0665-8 • $7.95pb • (757)

## *Proverbs & Love Poetry from Hippocrene . . .*

## St. Patrick's Secrets
## 101 Little-Known Truths and Tales of Ireland
*Helen Walsh Folsom*
*Illustrated by Fergus Lyons*
   Well now, have you heard about how the Irish fought for Alexander the Great? Or did you know that at one time the Irish were forbidden to wear trousers? Perhaps you don't know why the Irish revere John Paul Jones or how Jack the Ripper influenced Irish "Invincibles."
   *St. Patrick's Secrets*, with 101 curious, delightful, ironic and even outrageous tales from the Emerald Isle, is a must-have for every Irish-interest library. Illustrations by County Sligo native Fergus Lyons add style and humor to the collection.
150 pages • 5½ x 8½ • 0-7818-0898-7 • $12.95pb • (325)

## Irish Proverbs
*Illustrated by Fergus Lyons*
   A collection of wit and wisdom in the great oral tradition of Ireland makes this collection interesting and informative. Two hundred proverbs discuss the hard times, the good times and the great times experienced by the Irish people in the cities, out in the country, and by the sea. Also included are 30 illustrations from County Sligo artist Fergus Lyons, all of which add style and humor to the collection.
160 pages • 5½ x 8½ • 30 illustrations • 0-7818-0676-3 • $14.95hc • (761)

## Scottish Proverbs
*Illustrated by Shona Grant*
   Through opinions on love, drinking, work, money, law and politics, the sharp wit and critical eye of the Scottish spirit is charmingly conveyed in this one-of-a-kind collection. The proverbs are written in the colloquial Scots-English language of the turn of the century. Twenty-five witty and playful illustrations by Glasgow artist Shona Grant bring the proverbs to life for readers.
130 pages • 6 x 9 • 25 illustrations • 0-7818-0648-8 • $14.95 hc • W • (719)

## Treasury of Irish Love Poems, Proverbs & Triads
*edited by Gabriel Rosenstock*

This compilation of over 70 Irish love poems, quotations and proverbs spans 15 centuries and features English translations as well as poetry from such prominent Irish poets as Colin Breathnach and Nuala Ní Dhomhnaill. With selections exploring the realm of lost love, first love, and love's powerful grasp, discover why this book is essential to any Irish literature collection.

128 pages • 5 x 7 • 0-7818-06445 • $11.95hc • $11.95hc • (732)

## Irish Love Poems: Dánta Grá
*edited by Paula Redes*

A beautifully illustrated anthology that offers an intriguing glimpse into the world of Irish passion, often fraught simultaneously with both love and violence. For some contemporary poets this will be their first appearance in a U.S. anthology. Included are poets Thomas Moore, Padraic Pearse, W.B. Yates, John Montague, and Nuala Ni Dhomnaill.

Gabriel Rosenstock, famous poet and translator, forwards the book, wittily introducing the reader to both the collection and the rich Irish Poetic tradition.

176 pages • 6 x 9 • illustrated • 0-7818-0396-9 • $14.95 • (70)

## Scottish Love Poems
## A Personal Anthology
*edited by Lady Antonia Fraser*

Lady Antonia Fraser has selected her favorite poets from Robert Burns to Aileen Campbell Nye and placed them together in a tender anthology of romance. Famous for her own literary talents, her critical writer's eye has allowed her to collect the best loves and passions of her fellow Scots into a book that will find a way to touch everyone's heart.

253 pages • 6 x 9 • 0-7818-0406-X • NA • $14.95pb • (482)

Prices subject to change without prior notice. To purchase **Hippocrene Books** contact your local bookstore, call (718) 454-2366, email orders@hippocrenebooks.com or write to: HIPPOCRENE BOOKS, 171 Madison Avenue, New York, NY 10016. Please enclose check or money order, adding $5 shipping (UPS) for the first book and $.50 for each additional book. Visit us online: www.hippocrenebooks.com.

www.ingramcontent.com/pod-product-compliance
Lightning Source LLC
Jackson TN
JSHW011355130125
77033JS00023B/702